Beading All-Stars

20 Jewelry Projects from Your Favorite Designers

Marcia DeCoster

Jamie Cloud Eakin

Mabeline Gidez

Diane Hyde

Amy Katz

Rachel Nelson-Smith

Glenda Paunonen
and Liisa Turunen

Sherry Serafini

Melissa Grakowsky Shippee

Anneta Valious

LARK JEWELRY
& BEADING

LARK JEWELRY & BEADING

An Imprint of Sterling Publishing
387 Park Avenue South
New York, NY 10016

ISBN 978-1-4547-0862-9

Library of Congress Cataloging-in-Publication Data

Beading all-stars : 20 jewelry projects from your favorite designers.
    pages cm
  Includes index.
  ISBN 978-1-4547-0862-9
  1. Beadwork. 2. Jewelry making.
  TT860.B3339643 2014
  746.5--dc23
                              2013045134

Distributed in Canada by Sterling Publishing
c/o Canadian Manda Group, 165 Dufferin Street
Toronto, Ontario, Canada M6K 3H6
Distributed in the United Kingdom by GMC Distribution Services
Castle Place, 166 High Street, Lewes, East Sussex, England BN7 1XU
Distributed in Australia by Capricorn Link (Australia) Pty. Ltd.
P.O. Box 704, Windsor, NSW 2756, Australia

For information about custom editions, special sales, and premium and corporate purchases, please contact Sterling Special Sales at 800-805-5489 or specialsales@sterlingpublishing.com.

Email academic@larkbooks.com for information about desk and examination copies. The complete policy can be found at larkcrafts.com.

Every effort has been made to ensure that all the information in this book is accurate. However, due to differing conditions, tools, and individual skills, the publisher cannot be responsible for any injuries, losses, and other damages that may result from the use of the information in this book.

Manufactured in China

2 4 6 8 10 9 7 5 3 1

larkcrafts.com

Contents

Marcia DeCoster

Marcia DeCoster became acquainted with beads in the early 1990s and since that time has employed them as her primary artistic form to create beautifully wearable pieces of jewelry. Marcia's love of teaching beadwork has allowed her to travel broadly, both nationally and internationally, and she feels fortunate to count many beaders around the world as friends. She taught the Master Class at the 2013 Bead&Button Show. Marcia's work has been featured in *Masters Beadweaving*, *The Art and Elegance of Beadweaving*, and *500 Beaded Objects*, and has been included in many other bead publications. Her first book, called *Marcia DeCoster's Beaded Opulence*, released in 2009. Her more recent titles, *Marcia DeCoster's Beads in Motion* and *Marcia DeCoster Presents*, were released in 2013 and 2014, respectively. See more work, learn more about the artist, and view workshop dates on her website: www.marciadecoster.com.

SUPPLIES

Size 11° seed beads:

    A, silver, 14 g

    B, antique zinc (metal), 2 g

Size 15° seed beads:

    C, silver, 2 g

    D, dark gray matte, 0.5 g

    E, bright silver, 0.5 g

12 dark silver crystal bicones, 4 mm

2 dark silver crystal bicones, 3 mm

2 gray teardrop pearls, 8 mm

1 gray faceted diamond-shaped flat-backed crystal, 23 x 15 mm

FireLine, 6 lb. test

Wax

Size 12 and 13 needles, beading or sharps

Small, sharp scissors

DIMENSIONS

7 inches (17.8 cm) long, excluding clasp

TECHNIQUES

Cubic right angle weave (RAW)

Square stitch (page 123)

Deco Bracelet

With its steely color and geometric forms, this stunner captures the spirit of the Jazz Age. The clasp is a clever invention, consisting of a completely separate strip of narrow beadwork with large pearls at either end. You slide the clasp through each end of the band of the bracelet, then one pearl slips through the strip like a button through a buttonhole.

Make the Bracelet Bands

Think of a cube as a room. You will start a cube by making its floor. When you add three beads on the first side of the floor to begin creating the cube, two beads become part of the wall, with the bead in the center becoming the ceiling. You must add beads on each side of the floor to create the four walls. The ceiling beads of one cube become the next cube's floor beads. The contrasting beads become the earrings' outside edge.

When turning a corner to create an angle, the corner cube must have one contrasting ceiling B on the outside wall and one on the wall opposite it. Figure 5 shows the contrasting bead on the last cube before a turn where that cube's ceiling beads have the contrasting bead on only one wall. Figures 6 and 8 show the ceiling Bs in the corner cube where you create the angle. Cube 1 on the first band is also a corner cube, but since it is the first cube, only the opposing floor beads plus the ceiling bead on one wall are contrasting Bs.

CORNER CUBE, CUBE 1

1 Using a waxed, doubled length of FireLine, pick up one B, one A, one B, and one A, and tie them in a ring. Weave your thread through the beads to exit at a B bead.

2 Pick up one A, one B, and one A, and pass through the floor B again and the floor A (figure 1).

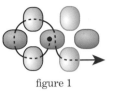

figure 1

3 Pick up two As and pass through the A on the side of wall 1 and through the floor A again and the floor B (figure 2).

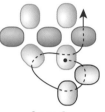

figure 2

4 Pick up two As and pass through the A in wall 2, the floor B again, the floor A, and the A on the side of wall 1 (figure 3).

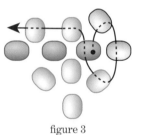

figure 3

5 Pick up one A and pass through the A in the side of wall 3, the floor A, the A in the side of wall 1, and the B in the ceiling of wall 1 (figure 4).

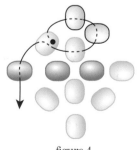

figure 4

CUBES 2 TO 9

Note: The ceiling in Cube 1 becomes the floor of Cube 2.

6 Continue as in steps 2 to 5, but for each cube, add one contrasting B as the ceiling bead only on the outside wall (wall 1).

CORNER CUBE, CUBE 10

7 As shown in figures 5 to 9, add a contrasting ceiling B on the outside wall and on the opposite wall. **Note:** Cube 10 turns a corner; to continue the line of Bs along the outside edge, the third wall must have a contrasting B bead as its ceiling, directly opposite the outside wall.

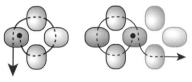

figure 5   figure 6

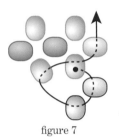

figure 7

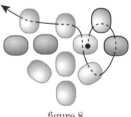

figure 8

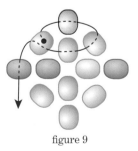

figure 9

To make the angle in the band, you must weave your thread through the beads to the edge bead on the inside wall of Cube 10 before starting Cube 11.

CUBES 11 TO 29

8 Complete as for Cubes 2 to 9.

CORNER CUBE, CUBE 30

9 Complete as for Cube 10. To make the angle in the band, weave your thread through the beads to the edge bead on the inside wall of Cube 30 before starting Cube 31.

CUBES 31 TO 49

10 Complete as for Cubes 2 to 9.

CORNER CUBE, CUBE 50

11 Complete as for Cube 10. To make the angle in the band, weave your thread through the beads to the edge bead on the inside wall of Cube 50 before starting Cube 51.

CUBES 51 TO 59

12 Complete as for Cubes 2 to 9.

CORNER CUBE, CUBE 60

13 Complete as for Cube 10.

14 Repeat steps 1 to 13 to make a second band.

Bezel the Flat-Backed Crystal

15 Thread an arm's length of single FireLine and use Cs to create a piece of cubic RAW that is 14 cubes long. Weave your thread through the beads to the side wall of the last cube and bead 11 more cubes. ***Note:*** Cube 14 is shared and becomes Cube 1 on Side 2. Cube 1 of Side 1 is also shared and becomes Cube 14 on Side 2. The join creates the 13th cube.

Position the last cube in line with the side wall of Cube 1 and join by

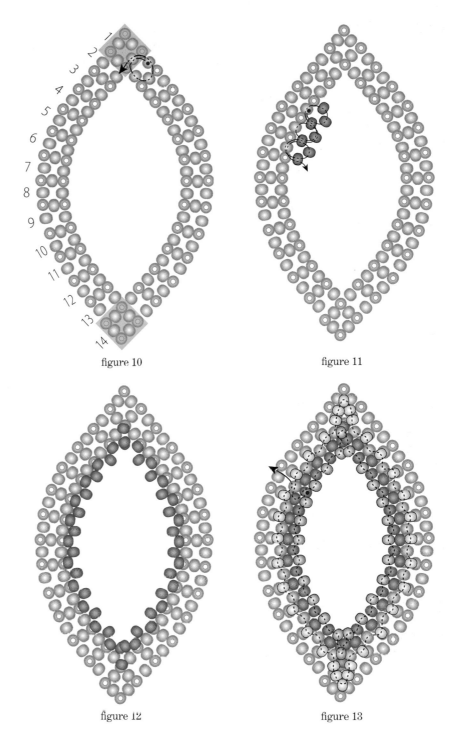

figure 10

figure 11

figure 12

figure 13

adding side beads on each of three walls. The fourth wall will have the sides already in place. Weave your thread through these four beads to reinforce the join (figure 10).

16 To embellish the bezel's interior, which will show on the bracelet's front, add three rounds of beads as follows.

Round 1. Weave your thread through the beads to a C on the inside edge of the cube, pick up three Ds, pass through the C again, and go up through the first D added. Continue with RAW in each of the edge's cube beads for the entire interior edge, as shown in figures 11 and 12.

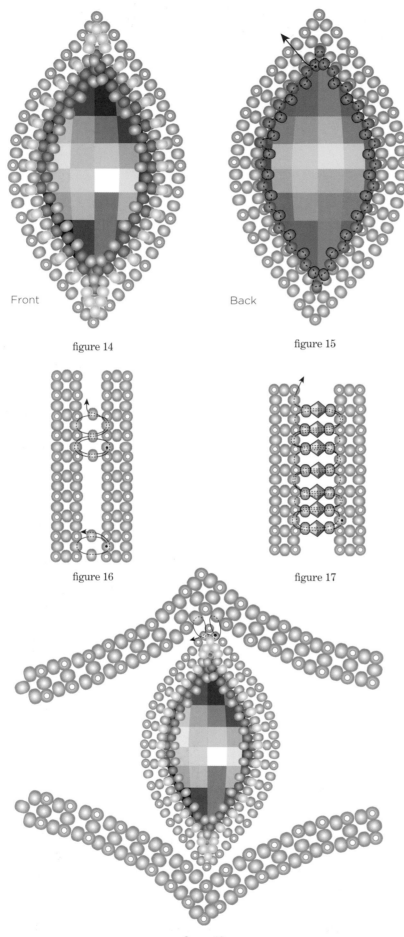

Front

Back

figure 14

figure 15

figure 16

figure 17

figure 18

Round 2. Refer to figure 13 as you work Rounds 2 and 3. Weave your thread through the beads to exit at an inside D on the edge of the RAW band just added. Pick up one C and pass through the next D. Repeat around.

Round 3. Weave your thread through the beads to exit at the C on the inside edge of the cube. Pick up one E and pass through the next C. At the ellipse's point on both ends, pick up five Es and pass through the next C.

17 Weave your thread through the beads to a C on the inside edge on the bezel's back. Insert the crystal from the back and position the front bezel over the crystal. Then secure the back as follows (figures 14 and 15).

Round 1. Working on the back while holding the crystal in place, pick up one D and pass through the next C all the way around.

Round 2. Repeat for a second row.

Connect the Bands

18 As shown in figure 16, use As to join the two bands at the front and back between the last two cubes on each end. Weave your thread through the beads to exit at the inside edge of the sixth cube from the end. Use As to join the two bands at the front and back between the sixth and seventh cubes from the end.

19 Weave your thread through the beads to exit at the inside edge of the 17th cube from the end. On the front only, pick up one A, one 4-mm bicone, and one A, and pass the thread through the inside bead on the opposite edge. Continue in RAW, using one A, one 4-mm bicone, and one A as the RAW units' top and bottom beads and the As on the edge of Cubes 17 to 22 on the two bands as the RAW units' side beads, for a total of seven groups of crystals (figure 17).

Attach the Bezeled Crystal

20 Weave a doubled thread through the bezel's beads and exit at an edge bead in one corner's cube. Pass through the bead on the band's inside edge at Cube 30 and back through the bead in the bezel, the adjacent bead in the bezel, and the adjacent edge bead on the inside of Cube 30. Reinforce by passing through the beads again. Repeat on the opposite side (figure 18).

Make the Clasp

Use a doubled length of waxed FireLine with a size 13 needle to ensure you'll be able to make all the required passes.

21 To begin square stitch, pick up four As and pass back through the first two beads. Adjust the beads to make them lie in two columns of two beads each.

22 Pick up two As, pass back through the first bead in the adjacent column, the first bead of the column you first exited, and the first bead just added (figure 19).

23 Pick up one teardrop pearl, one 3-mm bicone, and one C. Pass back through the 3-mm bicone, the pearl, and an A in one of the columns. Pass back up through the adjacent column and repeat the thread path to reinforce the join (figure 20).

24 Weave your thread through the beads to exit at the A bead at the bottom of a column. Pick up 22 As and pass through the first bead in the adjacent column, the bead you first exited, and the next 12 beads.

25 Pass through the 11th bead and pull to align beads 11 and 12 next to one another. Repeat the thread path to reinforce it (figure 21).

26 Pick up 2 As and pass through beads 12, 11, and the first bead just added (figure 22).

27 Continue in square stitch for 14 more rows.

28 Add a teardrop pearl at this end to match the other end. Pass the thread through the beads again to reinforce the join (figure 23).

To complete the clasp, push both ends of the strand with the teardrop pearls through the openings between the bands at each end of the bracelet; with the bands now held together by the strand, push the pearl on the square-stitched side through the opening in the two columns of beads that end with the other pearl.

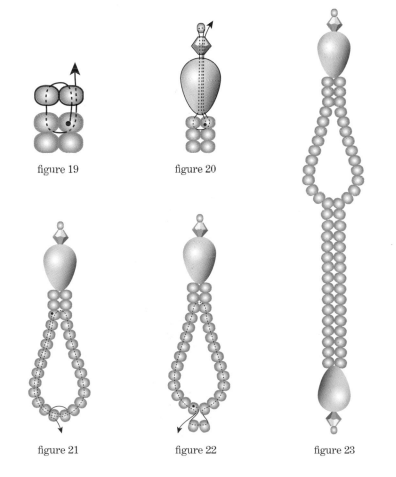

figure 19

figure 20

figure 21

figure 22

figure 23

SUPPLIES

Size 11° seed beads:
    A, dark silver, 5 g
    B, 48 dark gray matte

Size 15° seed beads:
    C, dark silver, 1 g
    D, 40 dark gray matte

48 dark silver round crystals, 3 mm

112 golden gray round crystals,
    2 mm

2 dark silver crystal bicones, 4 mm
    (optional)*

2 black ear wires with long
    unbent edge*

FireLine, 6 lb. test

Size 12 and 13 needles, beading
    or sharps

Small, sharp scissors

Round-nose pliers

Chain-nose pliers

* See step 17.

DIMENSIONS
2³/₄ inches (7 cm) long, including
    ear wire

TECHNIQUES
Cubic right angle weave (RAW)

INSTRUCTIONS

Create the Bottom Component

This component is made of 28 cubes, as follows. While you make the cubes, use figure 1 as your guide to their placement.

Think of a cube as a room. You'll start the first cube by making its floor. When you add three crystals on the first side of the floor to begin creating the cube, two crystals become part of the wall, with the crystal in the center becoming the ceiling.

Erté Earrings

Long, curvy, and graceful, these geometric earrings are named after an Art Deco master who specialized in glamorous and elaborate fashion design, but they move easily between dressed up or dressed down.

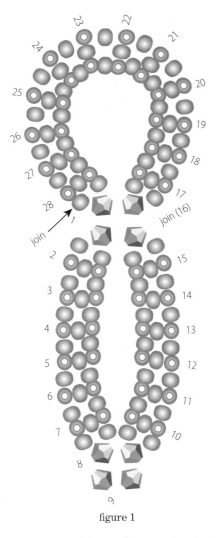

figure 1

3 Pick up three 3-mm crystals and pass through the floor crystal again and the next floor crystal (figure 2).

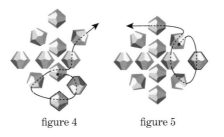

figure 2   figure 3

4 Pick up two 3-mm crystals and pass through the side crystal of wall 1, the floor crystal again, and the next floor crystal (figure 3).

5 Pick up two 3-mm crystals and pass through the side crystal of wall 2, the floor crystal again, the next floor crystal, and the side crystal of wall 1 (figure 4).

figure 4   figure 5

6 Pick up one 3-mm crystal and pass through the side crystal of wall 3, the floor crystal again, the side crystal of wall 1, and the ceiling crystal of wall 1 (figure 5).

CUBES 2 TO 7

7 Pick up one A, one B, and one A, and pass through the floor bead again and the next floor bead (figure 6). **Note:** The crystals shown in figure 6 are the ceiling beads of Cube 1. The floor beads, therefore, are crystals on Cube 2, but are 11°s on Cubes 3 through 7. Remember that the contrasting B is the outside edge of the ellipse.

Complete the cube using As and Bs, as shown in figures 7 to 9.

Repeat for Cubes 3 to 7.

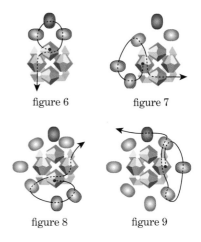

figure 6   figure 7

figure 8   figure 9

CUBE 8

8 Pick up one A, one 3-mm crystal, a crystal, and one A, and pass through the floor bead again, and the next floor bead (figure 10).

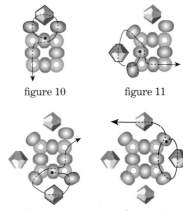

figure 10   figure 11

figure 12   figure 13

Complete the cube using As as the walls' sides and 3-mm crystals as the ceiling beads, as shown in figures 11 to 13.

CUBE 9

9 Complete as for Cube 1, using 3-mm crystals.

To move to the proper location to create the ellipse's point, weave your thread through the beads to exit at a crystal that lies on the side wall, opposite the edge of the cube that has the contrasting dark bead. This side is the inside of the ellipse. These four crystals become your new floor beads.

You must add crystals on each side of the floor to create the four walls. The ceiling beads of each cube become the floor beads of the next cube. The contrasting beads become the outside edges of the earring.

1 Thread an arm's length of doubled FireLine and wax it.

CUBE 1

This cube, complete with crystals, is at the center of the bottom component, where the circular and the elliptical parts meet, and you will use its walls to complete the ellipse and the circle.

2 Pick up four 3-mm crystals and tie them into a ring. These crystals are the cube's floor.

CUBES 10 TO 15

10 Complete as for Cubes 2 to 7.

CUBE 16

11 Add As to join Cube 15 to Cube 1. Weave your thread through the beads to exit at a crystal on Cube 1 at the top.

CUBES 17 TO 28

12 Complete as for Cubes 2 to 7.

Add As to join Cube 28 to Cube 1.

Embellish the Edges

13 Weave your thread through the beads to exit at an A on the outside edge where you completed the join. Pick up one 2-mm crystal and pass through the next A. Continue adding 2-mm crystals to the point of the ellipse in Cube 9. When exiting the crystal on the bottom edge of Cube 9, at the point, pick up 3 Cs and pass through the next crystal. Weave your thread through the beads to the component's opposite side and repeat the embellishment, adding 2-mm crystals along the other side of the ellipse and the circular part of the component (figure 14).

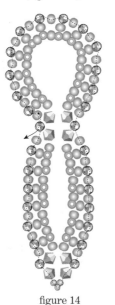

figure 14

Create a Ring at the Top

14 Use an arm's length of single FireLine to begin the cubic RAW. Pick up 3 Cs and 1 D and tie them in a ring. Weave your thread through the beads to exit at the D. *Note:* The contrasting Ds run along the circle's outside edge. Use the line of contrasting Ds to make sure that you don't twist the cubic RAW when you join the two edges to make the ring.

Complete 19 units of cubic RAW using Cs with a D on the ceiling of each cube's first wall. Insert this strip through the circular part of the bottom component (Cubes 17 to 28). Being careful to align the beads on the contrasting edge to place them opposite one another at the component's ends, add Cs to complete the join (figure 15).

figure 15

15 Weave your thread through the beads to exit at a contrasting D. Pick up one 2-mm crystal and pass through the next D. Repeat around the component for a total of 20 times. Weave your thread through the beads to exit at a ceiling bead.

16 Pick up seven Cs and pass through the opposite C. Reinforce the beadwork by passing your thread through the beads again and then weave your thread through the beads and cut it to complete the component (figure 16).

figure 16

17 You don't have to embellish your ear wires. If you choose to add a matching crystal, however, the ear wires will need to have one long unbent edge. Proceed as follows. Place a 4-mm crystal on the unbent edge. Using round-nose pliers, turn a loop in the wire (figure 17). Trim as necessary.

figure 17

Use chain-nose pliers to open the ear wire's loop and place the seven-bead loop on your earring's top through the open loop. Close the loop with the pliers.

18 Repeat all steps to make a second earring.

A Marcia DeCoster
Duomo's Romanticos, 2013
18 x 2.5 cm
Seed beads, Swarovski Elements
Photo by artist

B Marcia DeCoster
La Navette, 2013
18 x 6 cm
Seed beads, Swarovski Elements,
metal clasp
Photo by artist

C Marcia DeCoster
Robbin's Nest, 2013
20 x 9 cm
Fish leather, glass beads, enameled
filigree, Ultrasuede
Photo by artist

D

D Marcia DeCoster
Santa Lucia, 2013
41 cm long
Seed beads, Swarovski Elements,
metal clasp
Photo by artist

Jamie Cloud Eakin

Jamie Cloud Eakin has been a professional bead artist for almost two decades, and she teaches and sells her work in galleries across North America. She is the author of four books, including the best-selling *Beading with Cabochons*, and her latest, *Bead Embroidery Jewelry Projects*. Jamie lives in Modesto, CA. Her website is www.StudioJamie.com.

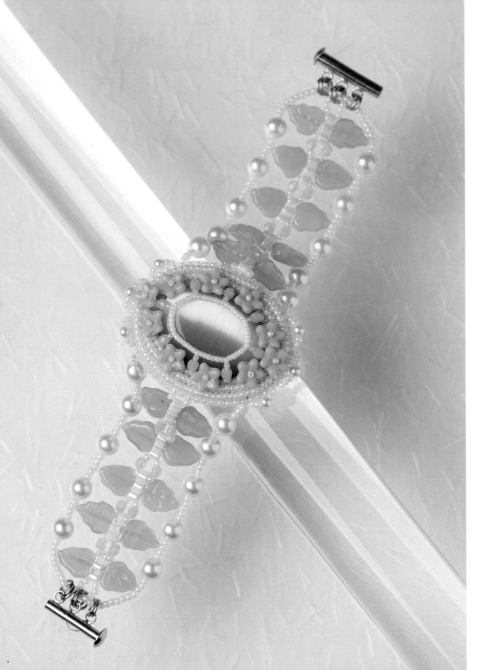

SUPPLIES

Opaque cream Ceylon size 8°
Delicas, 2 g

Light cream opaque luster size 11°
seed beads, 4 g

Light cream opaque luster size 15°
seed beads, 1 g

24–28 opal aqua Czech
fire-polished beads, 3 mm

10 turquoise opaque center-drilled
glass flower beads, 8 x 3 mm

20–24 green opal glass leaf beads,
10 x 7 mm

20–24 cream round pearls, 6 mm

6 cream round pearls, 3 mm

1 green cat's-eye glass cabochon,
30 x 22 mm

1 gold 3-hole slide clasp

12 gold jump rings, 5 mm

2¹/₂ x 2 inches (6.4 x 5.1 cm)
of backing

2¹/₂ x 2 inches (6.4 x 5.1 cm)
of outer backing

Cream or white size B thread

Size 12 beading needles

Chain-nose pliers

Craft adhesive

DIMENSIONS

7¹/₂ x 2 inches (19 x 5.1 cm)

TECHNIQUES

Bead embroidery (page 123)

Backstitch (page 124)

Stacks stitch (page 124)

Standard edge stitch (page 124)

Ladder stitch (page 122)

Flower Garden Bracelet

This piece of jewelry might have been inspired by French gardens, with their formal symmetry, harmonious colors, orderly rows, and central ornament. A seventeenth-century treatise on gardens à la française said their main function is to give the viewer aesthetic pleasure. Hasn't Jamie also fulfilled that objective with this bracelet?

INSTRUCTIONS

1 Mark vertical and horizontal lines that go through the backing's center. Glue the cabochon to the backing's center and let it dry.

Create a Window Bezel

2 The bezel is a window bezel on a base row.

Round 1. Stitch a row of 11°s around the cabochon using the 4-6 backstitch.

Round 2. Use the stacks stitch to position stacks as illustrated in figure 1. For each stack, use one 11°, one 3-mm fire-polished bead, and two 15°s, with the last 15° being the stopper. After the last stack, stitch up through the first stack, including the stopper bead.

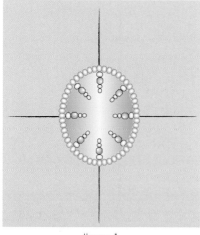

figure 1

Round 3. Pick up five to seven 15° beads each time, as needed to span the distance between stacks, and pass your thread through the next stack's stopper. Continue around the cabochon to the starting point, completing the bezel (figure 2). Pass your thread around the third round of beads several times to straighten and strengthen it, stopping next to a stack. Pass your thread down the stack to the beadwork's back.

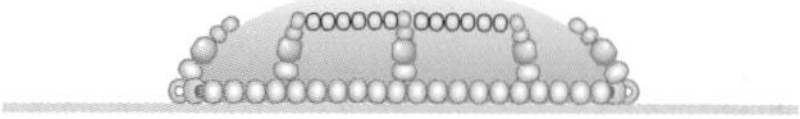

figure 2

Rounds 4 and 5. Stitch two more rows with 11°s, using the 4-6 backstitch.

Round 6. Embellish around the cabochon with the stacks stitch, using a flower for the stack and a 15° bead for the stopper. First, position a stack in the center of each window stitching up from the back side between the cabochon and the base row. Then add a stack at the cabochon's top and bottom, positioning the stack between the base row and additional row (figure 3).

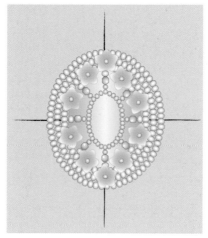

figure 3

3 Trim the backing close to the last row, being careful not to cut threads. Glue on the outer backing, let it dry, and trim it.

4 Stitch with 11°s around the edge using the standard edge stitch. Find and mark the center of the sides.

Add the Strap Sections

5 Cut 2 yards (1.8 m) of thread and put it on a needle to work as a single thread. Pass your thread through the backings from the back to the top, positioned at least ¼ inch (6 mm) from the edge and under an edge bead, leaving a 9-inch (22.9 cm) tail. Refer to figure 4 if the center is a bead, or follow figure 5 if the center lies between two beads. Stitch out through the edge bead. Pick up one 11°, one 8°, and one

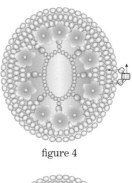

figure 4

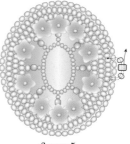

figure 5

11°. Then stitch down through the edge bead on the other side of the center, staying on the top. Stitch through the backings to the back, at least ¼ inch (6 mm) from the edge; then go out though the edge bead. Stitch through the 11° as well as through the 8°.

6 Using ladder stitch and 8°s, add ladder steps until there are four 8° beads.

7 Add another ladder stitch using one 11°, one 3-mm fire-polished bead, and one 11° bead for the sides with an 8° for the ladder step, as illustrated in figure 6.

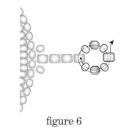

figure 6

8 Add two more ladder steps using 8°s.

9 Repeat steps 7 and 8 until you have the desired length. When sizing for your wrist, remember to factor in the end loop, jump rings, and clasp that you'll eventually add.

10 Create an end loop with eight 11°s (figure 7). Stitch through the loop two more times to reinforce it. Weave your thread back through the ladder's beads to the edge bead on the center section. Stitch down through the edge bead, staying on the top. Stitch through the backings to the back, at least ¼ inch (6 mm) from the edge; then go out through the edge bead.

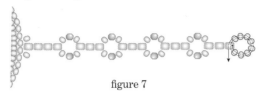

figure 7

11 Weave your thread through the ladder's beads to add the leaf fringe, as illustrated in figures 8 and 9, using a leaf and one 11° as the stopper bead. Add the leaf fringes across the bracelet's ladder section, then weave your thread back through the ladder's beads to return to an edge bead on the bracelet's center. Stitch through the edge bead and backings. Stitch over to the tail thread and use it to tie a square knot. Weave in the ends and cut.

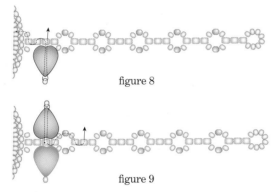

figure 8

figure 9

12 Cut 3 yards (2.7 m) of thread and put a needle on it. Move the needle to the center to work with doubled thread. Stitch your thread up from the back to the top, at least ¼ inch (6 mm) from the edge, and out through the edge bead that is the sixth bead from the ladder section thread (figure 10).

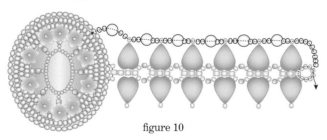

figure 10

Leave a 9-inch (22.9 cm) tail. Pick up two 11°s, one 6-mm pearl, and two 11°s, and stitch through the stopper bead on the first leaf fringe. Adjust the count of the first 11°s beads as needed to make the leaf stand up straight. Pick up two 11°s, one 6-mm pearl, and two 11°s and pass through the next leaf fringe. Repeat to the last leaf fringe. Pick up ten 11°s (or adjust the count as needed to fit) and stitch through the top two beads in the loop at the end of the ladder section. Stitch around the loop to reinforce it. Repeat in

reverse, adding beads to the bottom of the strap to return to the center section of the bracelet.

13 Stitch down through the edge bead, staying on the top. Stitch through the backings to the back, at least 1/4 inch (6 mm) from the edge; then go out through the edge bead. Weave your thread back through the row created in the previous step to return to the start. Stitch into the edge bead, staying on the top. Stitch through the backings to the back, at least ¼ inch (6 mm) from the edge. Stitch over to the tail thread and use it to tie a square knot. Weave in the ends and cut.

14 Repeat steps 5 through 13 on the other side.

Add the Edge

15 Identify the center top and bottom of the center section of the bracelet by counting the beads on the edge. The standard side petal edge is on a base of four edge beads, and uses one 15°, one 11°, one 3-mm pearl, one 11°, and one 15° to create the petal. Plan your starting and ending point to create three petals like the examples in figures 11 and 12. If the center is a bead, like in figure 12, the petal will instead be on a base of five beads, so adjust the beads for the petal to two 15°s, one 11°, one 3-mm pearl, one 11°, and two 15°s.

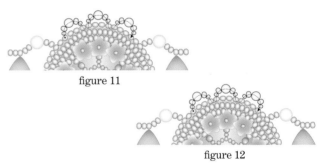

figure 11

figure 12

Cut 1 yard (91.4 cm) of thread and put on a needle to work single thread. Stitch your thread up from the back to the top, at least ¼ inch (6 mm) from the edge, leaving a 9-inch (22.9 cm) tail, and out through the edge bead. String the petal beads and stitch down through the edge bead on the other side of the petal, staying on the back. Stitch up to the top under that edge bead and at least ¼ inch (6 mm) from the edge. Stitch to the back, positioning the needle under the next edge bead and at least ¼ inch (6 mm) from the edge. Stitch out through the edge bead and create the next petal. After the last petal, weave the thread back through the edge and petal beads to return to the starting point. Use the tail thread to tie a square knot. Weave in the ends and cut it.

16 Repeat on the bottom edge.

Complete the Bracelet

Use the pliers and jump rings to attach the clasp.

SUPPLIES

Green metallic AB matte size 6°
    seed beads, 1 g

Light gray transparent luster size 8°
    seed beads, 1 g

Size 11° seed beads:
    Light gray transparent luster, 3 g
    Purple opaque rainbow, 7 g

Light gray transparent luster size 15°
    seed beads, 2 g

70 aventurine faceted round beads, 4 mm

26 aventurine faceted round beads, 6 mm

2 aventurine flat round carved rose beads,
    15 mm

72 lavender freshwater pearls, 8 mm

2 peace jade rondelle beads, 8 x 3 mm

4 metal rondelle flower spacers, 4 mm

42 aventurine round beads, 5 mm

13 lavender amethyst oval beads, 8 x 6 mm

36 peace jade rondelle beads, 6 x 3 mm

1 peace jade flat puffed oval bead,
    30 x 22 mm

74 peace jade round beads, 8 mm

8 silver crimp beads

2 pewter 5-hole connectors

1 pewter hook-and-eye clasp

22 silver jump rings, 5 mm

93 inches (2.4 m) of 0.018-inch (0.46 mm)
    flexible beading wire

Backing:
    5 pieces, 1¼ x 1¼ inches (3.2 x 3.2 cm)
    1 piece, 2 x 2¼ inches (5.1 x 5.7 cm)

Outer backing:
    5 pieces, 1¼ x 1¼ inches (3.2 x 3.2 cm)
    1 piece, 2 x 2¼ inches (5.1 x 5.7 cm)

Lavender size B thread

Craft adhesive

Size 12 beading needle

Small, sharp scissors

Crimping pliers

Wire cutter

Chain-nose pliers

DIMENSIONS
Longest strand, 29 inches (73.7 cm)

TECHNIQUES
Bead embroidery (page 123)

Backstitch (page 124)

One-bead stitch (page 123)

Stacks stitch (page 124)

Standard edge stitch (page 124)

Spring In Bloom Necklace

The architect who said "less is more" clearly hadn't discovered beads! If he had, he would have understood the desire beaders have to drape themselves in strand after strand of these beautiful baubles. Got that urge yourself? Here's the perfect project for it. Punctuate strings of lustrous pearls and semiprecious gems with textural pendants created with bead embroidery.

INSTRUCTIONS

1 You'll make the strands in order, from shortest to longest. Begin by cutting the beading wire into four pieces:

- one 17 inches (43.2 cm) long
- one 22 inches (55.9 cm) long
- one 24 inches (61 cm) long
- one 30 inches (76.2 cm) long

Make the Shortest Strand

2 String one 4-mm faceted aventurine and one gray 11° onto the 17-inch (43.2 cm) piece of beading wire. Repeat the bead sequence 62 more times. Add gray 11°s in equal numbers on each end of the strand until it measures 13¾ inches (35 cm).

> **TIP**
>
> Adding 11°s at both ends allows you to adjust the strand easily to get precisely the length you want while maintaining the pattern. Additionally, using the 11°s provides adequate space for the strands to hang properly, even when the part of the 5-hole connectors with the holes is narrower than the width of the five strands of beads. If you didn't use the 11°s, the first larger beads in each strand would not lie correctly.

3 On one end, add one gray 8°, one crimp bead, and nine gray 11°s. Insert the wire's end through the crimp bead and the 8° to create a loop (figure 1). Adjust the tension and crimp the crimp bead. Trim the beading wire. Repeat on the other end. **Note:** Make sure you don't have any slack in the strand before you crimp the other side. You don't want the wire to show, but you do want the

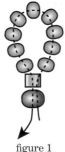

figure 1

beads to lie smoothly on your neck, without kinks in the strand.

4 Glue an aventurine rose bead to the center of one of the 1¼-inch (3.2 cm) backing pieces. Let the glue dry; then sew the bead to the backing using one-bead stitch.

Round 1. Using the 4-6 backstitch with purple 11°s, stitch a row around the rose bead.

Round 2. Add another row using the same stitch and beads as in Round 1.

> **TIP**
>
> Sometimes the rose bead's hole can show because it is elevated over the surrounding rows, but you can hide the hole with a bead. Stitch up from the back on the left side and stitch through the rose bead to the right. Pick up one 11° and stitch back through the hole (figure 2).
>
>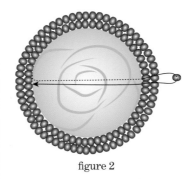
>
> figure 2
>
> Hold the bead and pull the thread to adjust the tension. Repeat on the other side. Stitch through the backing to the back.

5 Use the pearls and gray 11°s to create a clover stitch in the center of a second 1¼-inch (3.2 cm) backing piece. Here's how. As illustrated in figure 3, stitch one pearl (labeled with an A) onto the backing, then another pearl (B), and a final pearl (C). Repeat the thread path

again to strengthen the stitching. As shown in figure 4, stitch up through the backing to the outside of A. Stitch through A and pick up one 11° and stitch through C; then go down through the backing. Stitch up through the backing to the outside of B. Stitch through B, the 11°, and C, and stitch down through the backing. Stitch a row with purple 11°s around the clover using 2-3 backstitch. Fill in the gaps between the pearls with purple 11°s (figure 5).

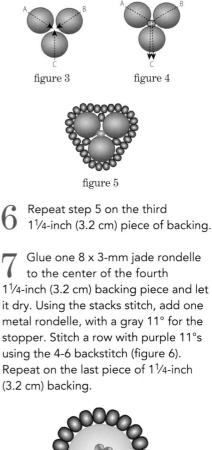

figure 3   figure 4

figure 5

6 Repeat step 5 on the third 1¼-inch (3.2 cm) piece of backing.

7 Glue one 8 x 3-mm jade rondelle to the center of the fourth 1¼-inch (3.2 cm) backing piece and let it dry. Using the stacks stitch, add one metal rondelle, with a gray 11° for the stopper. Stitch a row with purple 11°s using the 4-6 backstitch (figure 6). Repeat on the last piece of 1¼-inch (3.2 cm) backing.

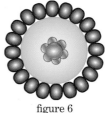

figure 6

8 Do the following on each of the components that you made in steps 4 to 7:

- Trim
- Then glue the outer backing on each piece and trim it.
- Finally, stitch the edge using purple 11°s and the standard edge stitch.

9 Arrange the pieces as illustrated in figure 7. Stitch the pieces together, combining two edge beads from each component (figure 8). Stitch through the backings and out through the edge bead on one component and through the edge bead on the other component. Stitch through the backings to the top side at least ¼ inch (6 mm) from the edge, then return to the back side, stitching through the backings under the next edge bead to connect. Repeat the thread path two more times.

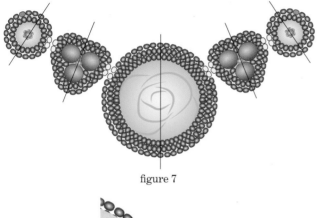

figure 7

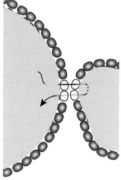

figure 8

10 Add an edge embellishment to the top of each of the five components, as illustrated in figure 9. Create these three-bead points as follows.

Stitch out through the edge bead, pick up three 15° beads, and stitch down into the next edge bead.

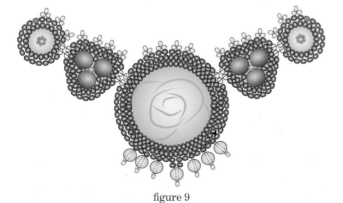

figure 9

Stitch up through the previous edge bead again, plus the 15° bead above it. Skip the middle 15° bead and stitch down through the third 15° bead and the edge bead below it, staying on the back side. Stitch through the backings to the top at least ⅛ inch (3 mm) from the edge.

Stitch to the back, positioning the needle under the next edge bead and at least ⅛ inch (3 mm) from the edge.

On the bottom of the center component, create fringes with the 4-mm faceted aventurines, using a 15° as the stopper.

11 Add a strand of beads for the neckpiece on each side of the combined section just made, as shown in figure 9. To do this, cut 2½ yards (2.3 m) of thread and put a needle on it to work it as a doubled thread. Add a stop bead with a 9-inch (22.9 cm) tail. String one purple 11° and one 5-mm aventurine. Repeat the bead sequence 20 more times; then add one purple 11°.

After stringing the beads, stitch through a bead on the combined section's outside edge, designated in green in figure 9, moving from the outside edge toward the beadwork and staying on the beadwork's top. Stitch under the beadwork and through the backings to the back, at least ¼ inch (6 mm) from the edge. Stitch out through the edge bead and through the entire strand of beads, removing the stop bead. Pick up purple 11°s until the length, from the center of the combined section to the end, measures 8 inches (20.3 cm). Add a needle to each of the tail threads and stitch through the added 11° beads.

12 Using the thread on the original needle, pick up one gray 8° and nine gray 11°s. Stitch through the nine 11°s again to create a loop (figure 10). Stitch each tail thread up through the 8° bead. Tie a square knot (page 120) using the working thread and the tail threads. Stitch down 2 inches (5.1 cm) into the bead strand with each tail thread and pull the knot into the 8°. Using the needle thread, stitch around the loop one more time. Then stitch down into the bead strand 2 inches (5.1 cm). Cut the threads.

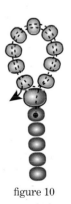

figure 10

13 Repeat steps 11 and 12 on the other side.

Make the Third Strand

14 Using the 22-inch (55.9 cm) beading wire that you cut in step 1, string on beads in the following pattern: one 6-mm faceted aventurine, one purple 11°, one amethyst, one purple 11°, one 6-mm faceted aventurine, one gray 11°, three 6 x 3-mm peace jades, and one gray 11°. Repeat the bead sequence 11 more times; then string on one 6-mm faceted aventurine, one purple 11°, one amethyst, one purple 11°, and one 6-mm faceted aventurine. Add purple 11°s in equal numbers at each end until the strand measures 18¾ inches (47.6 cm).

15 As you did in step 3, create a loop on each end of the strand, using one gray 8°, one crimp bead, and nine gray 11°s.

Make the Fourth Strand

16 Refer to figure 11 for this step and the next. Glue the 30 x 22-mm peace jade onto the remaining piece of backing, centered and ¾ inch (1.9 cm) down from the top. Glue on the second rose bead, centered and under the oval. Let the glue dry and stitch the beads to the backing using one-bead stitch. Stitch on one pearl on each side in the area between the rose and the jade and next to them using one-bead stitch.

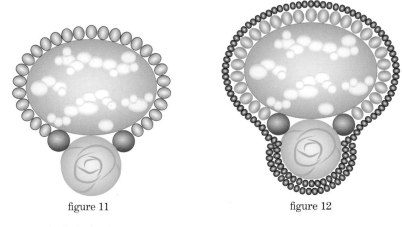

figure 11

17 Embellish the beadwork.

Round 1. Using the 4-6 backstitch, stitch around the peace jade with 6°s (figure 11).

Round 2. Refer to figure 12 for this round and the next. Stitch around the entire group with purple 11°s, using the 4-6 backstitch.

Round 3. Stitch around the rose-bead section again, using purple 11°s and the 4-6 backstitch.

figure 12

Round 4. Using 15°s and the 4-2 backstitch, stitch around the oval, beading between it and the inner round of 6°s and starting at one pearl and moving around the top to the pearl on the other side. Using the stacks stitch, add a metal rondelle for the stack and a 15° for the stopper, positioning them next to the two pearls as illustrated in figure 13, and as shown in the detail photo of the left side of page 23.

figure 13

18 Trim the backing. Glue the outer backing to the backing and trim it. Stitch the edge using purple 11°s and the standard edge stitch. Find and mark the center top.

19 Create a turn bead attachment at the component's center top using 8°s, referring to figure 14 if the center is a bead, or to figure 15 if the center is between two beads. Repeat the thread path three more times to reinforce the connection. Finish the rest of the edge with three-bead points using 15°s as described in step 10.

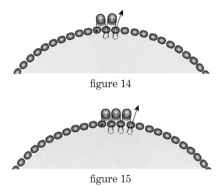

figure 14

figure 15

20 String the 24-inch (61 cm) piece of beading wire (cut in step 1) through the beads in the turn bead attachment and slide the piece of beadwork to the wire's middle. On one end of the wire, pick up one gray 11° and one pearl. Pick up one purple 11° and one pearl and repeat that bead sequence 30 more times. Repeat on the other end of the wire. Add purple 11°s in equal numbers at each end until the strand measures 20½ inches (52.1 cm).

21 As you did in step 3, create a loop on each end of the strand, using one gray 8°, one crimp bead, and nine gray 11°s.

Create the Longest Strand

22 String one 8-mm peace jade and one gray 11° onto the 30-inch (76.2 cm) beading wire cut in step 1. Repeat the bead sequence 73 more times. Add gray 11°s in equal numbers at each end until the strand measures 26¾ inches (68 cm).

23 As you did in step 3, create a loop on each end of the strand, using one gray 8°, one crimp bead, and nine gray 11°s.

Finish

24 Referring to the project photo, use chain-nose pliers to attach each strand in order to the 5-hole connectors, using two jump rings in each hole as shown in the photo directly above. Attach the halves of the clasp to each connector using jump rings.

> **TIP**
>
> If a strand is too short, you can add another set (or sets) of jump rings instead of remaking the strand. And if a strand is too long compared to the other strands, you can add jump rings to the other strands to lengthen them.

A

B

C

A **Jamie Cloud Eakin**
Coral Floral, 2013
16 x 11 cm
Coral/resin rosebuds, new jade, coral, patinated metal, seed beads; bead embroidery
Photo by artist

B **Jamie Cloud Eakin**
Beetle in a Bush, 2013
16 x 6 cm
Mosaic turquoise, dolomite scarab, tiger's-eye, wood, seed beads; bead embroidery
Photo by artist

C **Jamie Cloud Eakin**
Untitled Bracelets, 2013
Each, 17 x 4.5 cm
Acrylic flowers, cat's-eye glass, Czech glass, seed beads; bead embroidery, ladder stitch
Photo by artist

D **Jamie Cloud Eakin**
Zen Garden, 2013
14 x 8 cm
Chalk turquoise, coral, bone, seed beads; bead embroidery
Photo by artist

E **Jamie Cloud Eakin**
Frog on a Golden Pond, 2013
16.5 x 10 cm
Agate, lampwork glass, mother-of-pearl, pearls, Czech glass, metal, seed beads; bead embroidery
Photo by artist

D

E

Mabeline Gidez

Mabeline Gidez is a jewelry designer, beading instructor, and professional graphic designer. She has been creating distinctive, handcrafted jewelry for over 17 years, with more than 13 years of experience in teaching beading workshops all over the United States. Her keen eye for design and color, her presentation of step-by-step diagrams, and her patience all make her a highly sought-out instructor. She is the author of *I Can Right Angle Weave*. Although her favorite stitch is RAW, she does use a combination of stitches to create her pieces. Her signature style is her use of small beads and crystals. She finds inspiration in nature, food, fashion, movies, and diverse musical genres. Her art, reflecting both her interior and exterior worlds, speaks for itself. You can learn about Mabeline and see more of her work at www.MabelineDesigns.com.

SUPPLIES

Galvanized dusty orchid 8° seed
    beads, 2 g

Silver-lined medium pink size 11°
    seed beads, 3.5 g

Size 15° seed beads:

>   Semimatte silver-lined
>   lavender, 2.5 g

>   Galvanized silver, 2.5 g

1 off-white crystal pearl, 12 mm

39 rose crystal pearls, 3 mm

71 fuchsia AB2X crystal bicones,
    3 mm

87 light amethyst AB2X crystal
    bicones, 4 mm

2 violet round crystal beads, 8 mm

13 purple Rizo beads

White FireLine, 6 lb. test

Beeswax or microcrystalline wax

Size 12 needles, beading or sharps

Small, sharp scissors

Thread burner

1 bobbin for thread

DIMENSIONS

7³/₄ x 1³/₄ inches (19.7 x 4.4 cm)

TECHNIQUES

Tubular even-count peyote stitch
    (page 120)

Stitch in the ditch (page 121)

Netting

Flat spiral rope

Embellishing

Chrysa Bracelet

Mabeline has always been captivated by the beauty of the chrysanthemum and its concentric pattern of petals. The Chrysa is her beaded interpretation of this full blossom. It's a bejeweled and sparkly corsage, perfect for day or night! You can adapt this design easily into a pendant for a fancy necklace or an elegant brooch to adorn your favorite scarf in any season.

Create the Base of the Flower

1 Cut and wax 3 yards (2.7 m) of FireLine. Wrap 2 yards (1.8 m) onto the bobbin and leave 1 yard (91.4 cm) unwound, with a needle on its end. *Note:* The bobbin shows at the bottom of the illustrations on the left side.

2 String one 11°, the 12-mm pearl, and one 11°. Pass the thread back down through the pearl and through the first 11°, entering from the side opposite the one you exited.

3 Bead rows of peyote stitch to create a short tube around the pearl.

Rounds 1 and 2. String twelve 11°s. Pass through the 11° that you strung in step 2. These beads outline one side of the pearl. String another twelve 11°s. Pass through the very first 11° to outline the other side of the pearl (figure 1). *Note:* In tubular peyote stitch, the beads that you string become Rounds 1 and 2. For the next six rounds, each round uses 13 beads. Because you're stitching in even-count peyote stitch, you need to step up at the end of each round to come out of the first bead that you added in the current round.

figure 1

Round 3. Using one 11° for each stitch, peyote stitch around the pearl.

Round 4. Peyote stitch as in Round 3 (figure 2). *Note:* The illustration shows the beadwork as flat so that you can clearly see through which beads you need to pass; however, you're actually creating a beaded tube, where the new beads sit on top of the other beads, not a flat piece of peyote stitch.

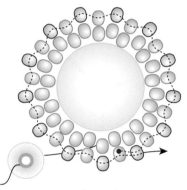

figure 2

Rounds 5 and 6. For both rounds, peyote stitch around the pearl, using one lavender 15° for each stitch. When you complete Round 6, do not exit out of a lavender 15°—in other words, don't step up. Pass the thread down through one 11° to the outside of the rounds of 15°s.

Round 7. Stitch in the ditch, adding one silver 15° for each stitch and passing the thread through one 11° in the round of 11°s (figure 3). *Note:* These 15°s actually sit on top of the round of 11°s. Pass the thread diagonally down one 11° to move to the next round below the current one.

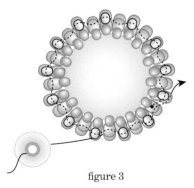

figure 3

Round 8. Working in the round of 11°s just below the round of silver 15°s that you just completed, string three lavender 15°s, skip one 11°, and pass through the next 11°. Stitch a round of netting around the ring to add a total of 13 units of netting (figure 4).

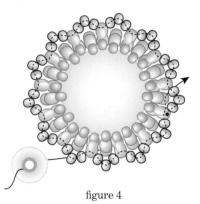

figure 4

Note: These lavender 15° picots actually sit beneath the round of 11°s to the outside of beadwork. Pass the thread diagonally through the next 11° of the next round.

Make the Stamens

4 Flip your beadwork to the back so that you can see the 11°s more easily. String three silver 15°s and one 11° and pass the thread back down through two silver 15°s. String one silver 15°, skip one 11° in the base (Round 1 from step 3), and pass through the next 11° (figure 5).

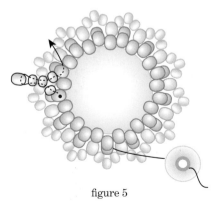

figure 5

Make 12 more stamens around the component, for a total of 13 stamens. Finish off your working thread by passing through a few beads until you find a place to tie a knot. Tie one half-hitch knot (page 120) between two beads. Continue to pass through a few more beads, moving away from your knot. Trim away excess thread with your scissors or a thread burner.

Add Rounds to the Base

In these rounds, you're going to add more rounds to the existing peyote tube to widen the beaded bezel around the pearl.

5 Unravel the thread from the bobbin and thread a needle onto it. Flip your beadwork to the back again and continue to work with the back of the flower facing up until otherwise specified. *Note: The next two rounds also each use 13 beads.*

Round 1. Passing through the 11°s of Round 1 from step 3, peyote stitch the round using one Rizo for each stitch and exiting out of the first Rizo added.

Round 2. Working in the Rizos that you added in Round 1 of this step, peyote stitch the round using one 11° for each stitch and passing through the holes at the top of the Rizos (figure 6). *Note: The 11°s in this round sit between the Rizos, on top of the beads from prior rounds.*

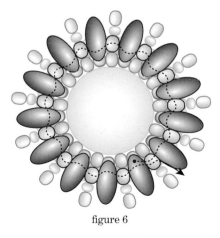

figure 6

Add Netting on the Edge

In the form of netting that this project uses, you'll always end a round by passing through the first few beads in the first unit of the current round to come out its center bead. For example, figure 7 shows that you would pass the thread up through the first two 11°s of the first unit of a round of netting to exit at its center 11° to place the needle in position to begin the next round. To create the next unit, you will always add the required beads and then pass the thread through the center bead of the next unit of netting in the prior round (figure 7).

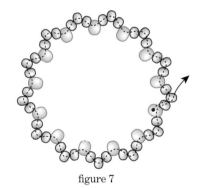

figure 7

6 As follows, create six rounds of netting, some of which use only one bead per unit. *Note: Each round contains 13 units of netting.*

Round 1. Add netting in this round, each time picking up three 11°s, skipping one Rizo, and passing the thread through the next 11° from Round 2 of step 5. *Note: Because you're working with the back of the flower facing up, this round of netting actually sits on top of the Rizos. The front of the component shows only the 15°s.*

Round 2. Add netting, using one 3-mm pearl for each unit (figure 8).

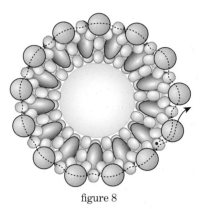

figure 8

Round 3. Add netting, using one 11° for each unit. When you're done, you should be exiting a 3-mm pearl.

Round 4. Add netting, using three silver 15°s for each unit. This round of netting sits behind the 11°s that you added in Round 3 of this step, between the 3-mm pearls and above the center 11°s of the netting added in Round 1 of this step (figure 9).

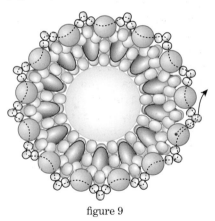

figure 9

Round 5. Add netting, using one 3-mm pearl, one silver 15°, and one 3-mm pearl for each unit.

Round 6. Add netting, using one lavender 15°, one 3-mm bicone, one lavender 15°, one 3-mm bicone, and one lavender 15° for each unit.

Add Petals to the Flower

7 Flip your flower to work the petals from the front.

Petal 1. Follow along with figure 10. With your thread coming out of the center silver 15° from Round 5 of step 6, string one lavender 15°, one 4-mm bicone, and one lavender 15°. Then pass through the 11° at the tip of the stamen made in step 4, directly below your current location toward the center of the component. String one lavender 15° and pass the thread back through the 4-mm bicone that you just added. String one lavender 15° and pass through the silver 15° from the netting that you made in Round 5 of step 6, where you initially started the current round. Then pass through the first lavender 15° of the first unit of netting in Round 6 of step 6, which is next to a 3-mm bicone in that same unit. String four lavender 15°s, skip over that 3-mm bicone, and pass through the center lavender 15° in that same unit.

String five lavender 15°s and form a circle by passing the thread through the last of the four beads that you strung before you passed through the center lavender 15°. Then pass through the center lavender 15° again and through the first lavender 15° of the five beads that you just added. String three lavender 15°s, skip over the 3-mm bicone from the first unit of netting in Round 6 of step 6, and pass through the next lavender 15° of that same unit and through the silver 15° from the netting made in Round 5 of step 6. One petal is complete.

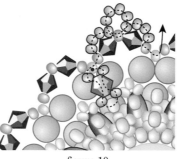

figure 10

Petals 2 to 13. Repeat the steps for petal 1 twelve more times. After making the last petal, exit out of one lavender 15° only; do not pass through the silver 15° from the netting made in Round 5 of step 6.

Points of the petals. Pass over the silver 15° from the netting made in Round 5 of step 6 and, in the first petal that you made, go up the first six lavender 15°s. String one lavender 15°. Pass the thread down through the next six lavender 15°s. This stitching adds a point to the petal (figure 11).

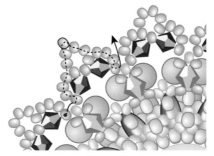

figure 11

Add points to the rest of the petals around the edge of the flower. Finish off your working thread by making a half-hitch knot, passing the thread through some beads, and trimming the thread. **Note:** By going through all of the petals and adding points to them, you're reinforcing them and making their shape more defined. The petals may start to ruffle a little, which is the desired effect.

Make the Strap on One Side

You make the strap in flat spiral rope.

8 Cut and condition 3 yards (2.7 m) of FireLine. Wrap half of the thread onto the bobbin and thread a needle. Flip your flower to the back and pass the thread through an 11° on the outside edge next to one of the pearls, moving from left to right. Leave the bobbin hanging at left.

9 String three 11°s, skip one 3-mm pearl, and pass through the next 11°. Repeat the same bead sequence once more.

10 String two 4-mm bicones, two silver 15°s, one 11°, one lavender 15°, one 8°, one lavender 15°, one 11°, and two silver 15°s. Pass the thread up through the two 4-mm bicones. Fold the D-shaped loop to the side opposite the bobbin. String two silver 15°s, one 11°, one lavender 15°, one 3-mm bicone, one lavender 15°, one 11°, and two silver 15°s. Pass the thread up through the 11° that is next to the first 4-mm bicone that you strung in this step and through the two 4-mm bicones.

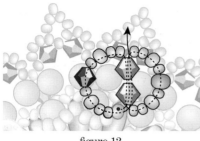

figure 12

Fold this new D-shaped loop to the same side as the bobbin (figure 12).

11 String one 4-mm bicone. String two silver 15°s, one 11°, one lavender 15°, one 8°, lavender 15°, one 11°, and two silver 15°s and pass the thread up through the top two 4-mm bicones. Fold this D-shaped loop so that it lies on top of the first loop on the right side, the one that also used an 8°. String two silver 15°s, one 11°, one lavender 15°, one 3-mm bicone, one lavender 15°, one 11°, and two silver 15°s. Pass up through the same two 4-mm bicones. Fold this D-shaped loop on top of the first one on the left side, the one that also used a 3-mm bicone (figure 13).

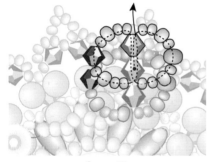

figure 13

12 Repeat step 11 until you've reached the desired length to complete the first half of the first side of your strap of the bracelet. **Note:** Make sure that your D-shaped loops with 3-mm bicones are all on one side, and the loops with the 8°s are on the opposite side.

13 Add a bead for the clasp. Pass through the two silver 15°s sitting above and to the right of the last 4-mm bicone. String three 11°s, one 8-mm crystal, and three silver 15°s, and pass the thread back down through the 8-mm crystal and one 11°. String two 11°s and pass the thread through all four silver 15°s sitting above the last 4-mm bicone, moving first through the two 15°s above and to the left of the bicone and then through the two 15°s to their right to form a triangle. Pass once more through all of the beads in this part of the clasp to reinforce the stitching. When you're done, finish off your working thread by making a half-hitch knot, passing the thread through some beads, and trimming the thread.

14 Unravel the FireLine from the bobbin, condition it if needed, and thread a needle. String two 4-mm bicones, two silver 15°s, one 11°, one lavender 15°, one 8°, one lavender 15°, one 11°, and two silver 15°s. Pass up through the two 4-mm bicones. Fold the D-shaped loop to the side opposite the 3-mm bicones on the first side of the strap. String two silver 15°s, one 11°, and one lavender 15° and pass the thread through the 3-mm bicone in the first unit on the completed side of the strap. String one lavender 15°, one 11°, and two silver 15°s. Pass through the 11° that is next to the first 4-mm bicone that you strung in this step and through the two 4-mm bicones (figure 14).

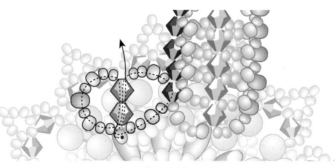

figure 14

15 String one 4-mm bicone, two silver 15°s, one 11°, one lavender 15°, one 8°, one lavender 15°, one 11°, and two silver 15°s. Pass up through the top two 4-mm bicones. Fold this D-shaped loop on top of the first loop that used an 8°. String two silver 15°s, one 11°, and one lavender 15°. Pass the thread through the next 3-mm bicone. String one lavender 15°, one 11°, and two silver 15°s. Pass the thread up through the same two 4-mm bicones. Make sure this new loop is on top of the first loop that used a 3-mm bicone.

16 Repeat step 15 until you've made this strap the same length as the first.

17 Repeat step 13 to add another bead for the clasp. You've now completed the strap on one side of your bracelet.

Create Loops for the Clasp

18 Create a beaded loop for the clasp as follows. Cut and condition 1 yard (91.4 cm) of new FireLine and thread a needle. String one 11° to use as a stop bead. Slide it down so it's 8 inches (20.3 cm) from the other end.

19 Work a tube using peyote stitch.

Rounds 1 and 2. Follow along with figure 15. String eighteen 11°s. Pass through the first two 11°s to form a base. **Note:** The strung beads become Rounds 1 and 2.

Round 3. Working in a tube, not outward, peyote stitch the round, using one 11° for each stitch. When you've completed this round, do not step up. **Note:** In the first three rounds and the fifth round, each round uses nine beads. Don't pinch your beadwork flat! It should form a short tube, not a flat disk.

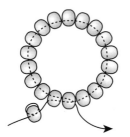

Rounds 1 and 2 added

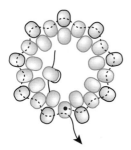

Round 3 added

figure 15

Round 4. Use three lavender 15°s for each stitch in this round. These beads will embellish your peyote stitch band and form little picots around it. When you complete the round, step up through an 11° from the third round in this step.

Round 5. Using one 11° for each stitch, peyote stitch the round. When you've completed the round, do not step up.

20 Pass the thread counter-clockwise through one 11°, three lavender 15°s, one 11°, three lavender 15°s, one 11°, and two lavender 15°s. You're now exiting the center 15° of three lavender 15°s that you added in round 4 of step 19. String one silver 15° and one 3-mm bicone and, moving clockwise, pass the thread through the center 15° of the next group of three lavender 15°s. String one 3-mm bicone and one silver 15°. Change direction and, moving counter-clockwise, pass the thread through the center 15° of the next group of three lavender 15°s, as shown in figure 16. Later, these two 3-mm bicones will be connected to the strap of the bracelet. Using the remaining thread, pass through all the beads that you just added again to reinforce the stitching. Finish off your working thread by making a half-hitch knot, passing the thread through some beads, and trimming the thread.

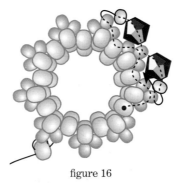

figure 16

21 Remove the stop bead and thread a needle onto the tail. Pass the thread through one 11° and two lavender 15°s to exit at the center 15° of the three lavender 15°s that you added in round 4 of step 19. String one 3-mm bicone, one silver 15°, and one 3-mm bicone, and pass the thread through the center 15° of the next three lavender 15°s (figure 17). When you're done, finish off your working thread by making a half-hitch knot, passing the thread through some beads, and trimming the thread. The loop is finished.

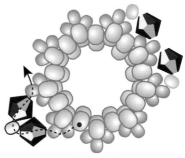

figure 17

22 Repeat steps 18 to 21 to make another loop for the clasp.

Make the Strap on the Other Side

23 Start the strap of the bracelet for the other side of the flower by cutting and conditioning 3 yards (2.7 m) of FireLine. Wrap half of the thread onto the bobbin and thread the needle. Flip your flower to the back. Pass through the fourth protruding 11° in the back of the flower. These 11°s lie between the 3-mm pearls (figure 18). *Note:* The first double-wide strap attaches to three of the protruding 11°s from the back of the flower. The second double-wide strap also attaches to three protruding 11°s from the back of the flower. Try to position the second strap directly across from the first. Both straps take up six out of the 13 protruding 11°s, leaving seven protruding beads. After adding the straps, you should have three unattached, protruding 11°s on one side, and four on the other.

Repeat steps 9 to 12 to make the first half of this strap for the unfinished side of the bracelet.

figure 18

24 To attach the beaded loop for the clasp, pass through the two silver 15°s next to the 3-mm bicone, moving from right to left. String one 11°. Moving to the clasp, pass through one 3-mm bicone, string one lavender 15°, and pass the thread through the next 3-mm bicone. String one 11° and pass the thread through the four silver 15°s above the 4-mm bicone at the end of the strap, moving from right to left, to form a square (figure 19). Use your remaining thread to reinforce this connection. When you're done, finish off your working thread by making a half-hitch knot, passing the thread through some beads, and trimming the thread.

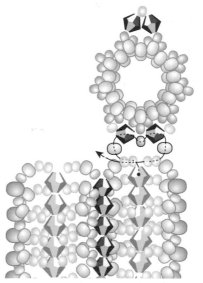

figure 19

25 Unravel the thread from the bobbin. Thread a needle and condition the thread if necessary. Repeat steps 14 to 16 to attach the other half of the second side of the strap of the bracelet. Repeat step 24 to add the other clasp.

SUPPLIES

Green/red gold luster size 11°
    Japanese seed beads, 2.5 g*

Galvanized gold size 15° seed
    beads, 2.5 g

2 light aqua/green rivolis, 12 mm

46 jet AB2X crystal bicones, 3 mm

36 matte olive green Japanese
    drop beads, 3.4 mm

2 gold-filled ear wires

Gray FireLine, 6 lb. test

Beeswax or microcrystalline wax

Size 12 needles, beading or sharps

1 thread bobbin

Small, sharp scissors

Thread burner

* Avoid using seed beads that are
    either too skinny or too wide
    and bulky.

DIMENSIONS

2¹⁄₄ x 1¹⁄₂ inches (5.7 x 3.8 cm)

TECHNIQUES

Tubular even-count peyote stitch
    (page 120)

Stitch in the ditch (page 121)

Netting

Cubic right angle weave (RAW)

Flat herringbone stitch

Mystic Sun Earrings

The sun plays a very important part in nature and has been honored in history by many cultures. The Incans worshipped it and were known for their precision in stonework architecture. These earrings pay homage to the building skills of their civilization and culture, as well as to the sun itself. Instead of using blocks of stone, Mabeline constructed these medallions with tiny beads that nestle together perfectly to form sparkling jewels.

INSTRUCTIONS

Create the Bezel

1 Cut 6 feet (1.8 m) of FireLine. Wrap 50 inches (1.3 m) of it onto the bobbin. Thread a needle onto the remaining 22 inches (55.9 cm) and condition it if desired.

Rounds 1 and 2. String on 28 size 11°s. Slide them down next to the bobbin and pass the thread through the first two 11°s to form a ring. **Note:** In tubular peyote stitch, these strung beads become the first and second rounds.

In the bezel, each round will use 14 beads. At the end of each round, you need to step up to come out the first bead that you added in the current round.

Round 3. Peyote stitch the round using one 11° for each stitch and making sure to exit out the side of the bead that is opposite where your bobbin thread is exiting (figure 1). *Note:* For clarity, the illustration shows the beads going outward around the ring, but you actually want the beads to sit on top of one another to create a tube. Make sure you're beading tightly enough that your tube fits snugly around the rivoli. The figure shows the bobbin at lower left.

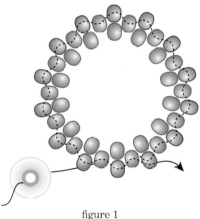

figure 1

Round 4. Repeat Round 3.

Round 5. Peyote stitch the round, using one 15° for each stitch.

Round 6. To finish the back of bezel, peyote stitch the round using one 15° for each stitch. To end your thread, pass your needle through a few beads until you find a place where you want to tie a knot. Tie a half-hitch knot (page 120) and pass the thread through a few beads, weaving away from the knot. Trim away any excess thread with scissors or a thread burner.

Start the Sunburst Medallion

2 Unwind the thread from the bobbin. Thread a needle and condition the thread if desired. Place the rivoli, foiled side down, facing toward the beadwork from the previous step. Hold it in place with one hand while you work with the other to trap the rivoli to complete the front of the beaded bezel, as follows.

Rounds 1 and 2. Peyote stitch two rounds, using one 15° for each stitch. Do not step up between these two rows of 15°s but rather pass through the same 11°s in the second round as you passed through in the first round (figure 2). *Note:* The beads in Round 2 will sit behind the beads in Round 1. The rivoli is now trapped within the bezel, and you don't need to hold it in place anymore. Pass the needle down diagonally through the next 11° in the next round below the current one, which originally was a bead in your initial ring of 28 beads. You are now moving from the front of the bezel toward its middle.

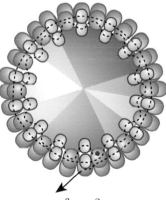

figure 2

Round 3. Now you'll be working on the outside edge of the rivoli. Stitch in the ditch using one drop bead for each stitch and passing through each 11° in the round. You should have 14 drop beads in the round when you're done.

Then pass the thread diagonally down through the next 11° in the next round below the current one, moving toward the other side of the bezel (figure 3).

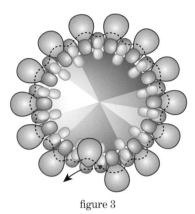

figure 3

Add Netting to the Medallion

In the form of netting that this project uses, you always end a round by passing through the first few beads in the first unit of the current round to come out its center bead. For example, in Round 1 in step 3, you must pass the thread up through the first two 15°s of the first unit of netting in the current round to exit at the center 15° of that same unit to start the next round.

3 As follows, add four rounds of netting and embellish the netting in Rounds 5 and 6.

Round 1. Flip your beadwork to the back. Add netting in this first round, each time stringing three 15°s and passing through an 11° from the round of 11°s to which you moved in Round 3 of step 1 (figure 4).

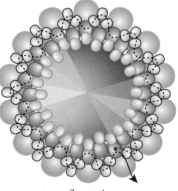

figure 4

Round 2. First step up by passing through the next two 15°s, to exit out of the center 15° in the first unit of the previous round. Add netting again using three 15°s for each unit.

Round 3. First step up by passing through the next two 15°s, to exit out of the center 15° in the first unit of the prior round. Add netting, stringing one 15°, one 11°, and one 15° for each unit (figure 5).

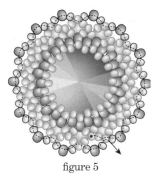

figure 5

Round 4. First step up by passing through one 15° and one 11°, to exit out of the center 11° in the first unit of the previous round. Add netting, stringing five 15°s for each unit (figure 6). After completing this round, do not step up. **Note:** Your thread should be coming out of the center 11° from round 3.

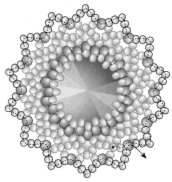

figure 6

Round 5. Flip your beadwork to the front. String one 15°, one bicone, and one 15° for each stitch and pass through the center 11° in each netting unit from Round 3 again (figure 7). **Note:** The crystals should sit on top of the center 15°s that you added in the last round.

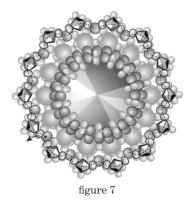

figure 7

Round 6. First step up by passing through the first two 15°s added in Round 4. Using three 15°s, skip the center 15° in Round 4 and pass the thread down through the next two 15°s in the same unit. Pass the thread through the next 11° from Round 3, and then pass the thread through the first two 15°s in the next unit of netting from Round 4. Repeat adding three 15°s around the rivoli. This stitching adds a more defined point to all of the units of netting (figure 8).

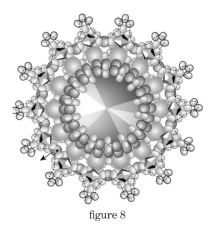

figure 8

Make the Clover Flower

You'll make this flower using cubic right angle weave. This component rests between the sunburst medallion and the ear wire.

4 First step up by passing through the next 15° in the pointed unit that you added in Round 6 of step 3. String one 15°, one bicone, and one 15° and, moving counterclockwise,

pass the thread down through the last 15° of Round 6 from step 3 and through the two 15°s on the side of the last unit of Round 4 from step 3 until you reach the 11° added in Round 3 of step 3. Pass through the 11° and up through the next three 15°s, two from the side of the unit from Round 4 of step 3 and one from the side of the netted point that you created in Round 6 of step 3. Continue to pass through the first 15° and the bicone that you strung in this step (figure 9).

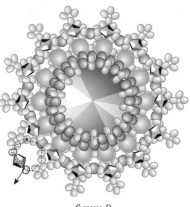

figure 9

5 String three 15°s, one bicone, three 15°s, one bicone, three 15°s, one bicone, and three 15°s, and pass the thread through the bicone that you strung in step 4 and the first 15° from the current step, to form a square.

6 String one bicone, one drop bead, and one bicone. Moving clockwise, pass the thread through the 15° on the other side of the bicone added in step 4 and then through the bicone itself, and through the next 15° in the square to form a triangle (figure 10).

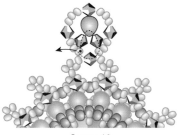

figure 10

7 In the square, pass the thread through the next two 15°s, one bicone, and one 15°. String one bicone and one drop bead and pass the thread through the bicone on the side of the first triangle. Then pass through the 15° on the near side of the next bicone in the square, the bicone itself, and the next 15° in the square to attach the second triangle (figure 11). Repeat this procedure one more time to attach a third triangle.

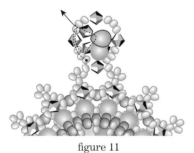

figure 11

In the square, pass through the next two 15°s, one bicone, and one 15°. To add the fourth triangle, pass up through one bicone on the side of the first triangle and string one drop bead. Pass down through one bicone on the side of the third triangle and then pass through the 15° on the near side of the next bicone, the bicone itself, and the next 15° in the square. Then pass up through one bicone and one drop bead in the first triangle (figure 12).

figure 12

8 At the top of the four large triangles, string one 15°, one bicone, and one 15°. Pass the thread through the same drop bead to form a small triangle. In the small triangle, pass up through the first 15° and through the bicone to the top of the small triangle. String one 15° and pass the thread through the drop bead directly across from the first small triangle. String one 15° and pass through the bicone from the first small triangle—now the top of the component—to create a second triangle and complete an X-shaped embellishment. Then pass through one 15° and one drop bead (figure 13). String one 15° and pass through the next drop bead. Repeat 3 more times to insert one 15° between each of the four drop beads to tighten up the clover of drop beads and hide any gaps where thread is showing.

figure 13

9 Pass the thread down to the square by going down through one bicone in the large triangle and through one 15° and one bicone in the square. String four 15°s and pass the thread through the same bicone from the square to encircle it. Then pass through the first two 15°s after the bicone (figure 14).

figure 14

Bail

You'll make the bail in herringbone stitch.

10 String two 15°s and pass the thread down through the next two 15°s, one bicone, and up three 15°s.

11 String two 15°s and pass the thread down through the next 15°. Pass your thread underneath the thread between the two 15°s directly above the bicone. Pass the thread back up through the top two 15°s on the same side (figure 15). Repeat this procedure once more.

figure 15

12 String seven 15°s and pass the thread down through the next 15°. String one 11° and pass the thread up through the next 15° on the other side next to the seven 15°s that you just added (figure 16). Pass the thread through all seven 15°s in the loop again to reinforce it. Finish off the remaining thread. Hook the bail into the loop of the ear wire.

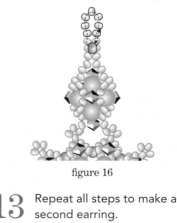

figure 16

13 Repeat all steps to make a second earring.

B

C

A **Mabeline Gidez**
Gwendoline Bracelet, 2012
18.5 x 2 cm
Swarovski pearls, Swarovski bicones,
silver-plated sliding bar clasp, thread; right
angle weave, embellished
Photo by artist

B **Mabeline Gidez**
Flora Pendant, 2013
4 cm in diameter
Swarovski rivoli, Delica beads, Japanese seed
beads, Swarovski bicones, Swarovski pearls,
Chinese crystals, silver, thread; tubular peyote
stitch, netting, wire wrapping
Photo by artist

C **Mabeline Gidez**
Elizabeth Bracelet, 2012
24.5 cm long
Glass pearls, Japanese seed beads, Swarovski
crystals, thread; cubic right angle weave, right
angle weave, circular and flat peyote stitch,
embellished
Photo by artist

Diane Hyde

Diane Hyde has been making things since she was a very young girl. She has always loved the process of dreaming up a design—a doll, a piece of jewelry, a thing—then getting down to the creative business of how to bring it to life. She thinks there's nothing better!

Her background is in graphic art and freelance illustration, but she has made and sold jewelry, wearable art, dolls, and purses since the late 1970s. For many years, she offered a vintage-look line of jewelry at fine art shows in the Midwest under the label Diane H. Designs. Her designs appeared in numerous galleries, in Von Maur department stores and Nordstrom trunk shows, in a nationally distributed San Francisco-based mail order catalog, and, in more recent years, in many published magazine articles and books.

Diane discovered beading in 1995, and she hasn't looked back since. Her focus lately is to incorporate bead embroidery and woven beading stitches with unexpected found objects. The goal is to impart a feeling of Victorian and other vintage styles, and she especially loves it when there's an added air of quirkiness, mystery, and the unexpected within her creations. Visit www.dianehyde.com.

SUPPLIES FOR THE WRAPPING PAPER COMPONENT

Matte brown size 8° seed beads, 1 g

Size 11° seed beads:

    Mottled green, 1.5 g

    Light bronze, 0.5 g

Size 15° seed beads:

    Light bronze, 0.5 g

    Matte light olive, 0.5 g

4 soldered jump rings, 5 mm

1 piece of beading foundation,
    2 x 2$^1/_2$ inches (5.1 x 6.4 cm)

1 piece of medium green synthetic
    suede, 1$^3/_4$ x 1$^1/_2$ inches
    (4.4 x 3.8 cm)

Nylon thread:

    Brown

    Neutral

1 rectangular brass (or cardboard)
    blank, 1$^1/_4$ x $^{15}/_{16}$ inch (3.2 x 2.4 cm)

1 image of a pinecone, 1$^{15}/_{16}$ x 1$^1/_4$ inch
    (4.9 x 3.2 cm) or smaller*

2 sheets of white paper

Size 10 needles, beading or sharps

Small, sharp scissors

Paper scissors

Pencil

Newspaper

Cutting mat

Craft knife

Ruler

Steel wool

Soap

Burnisher (optional)

Spray adhesive

Clear polyurethane spray sealant,
    gloss or matte, for digital images

Craft adhesive

* Diane used wrapping paper left over
   from the holidays.

DIMENSIONS

1$^5/_8$ x 1$^1/_4$ inches (4.1 x 3.2 cm)

TECHNIQUES

Bead embroidery (page 123)

One-bead stitch (page 123)

Backstitch (page 124)

Whipstitch (page 123)

Whispering Pines Necklace

A tiny pinecone collected on a walk years ago, some old holiday wrapping paper found in the attic, and a small fragment from a ceramic tea set that Diane owned as a child—all come together to create a unique, themed keepsake. You can choose to make your necklace with the three components shown, or simplify and make just one to wear as a pendant.

INSTRUCTIONS FOR THE WRAPPING PAPER COMPONENT

1 Protecting your work surface with newspaper, place the image of the pinecone face down on it and apply spray adhesive to the back. Adhere the image to a sheet of white paper, smooth out the paper by pressing it firmly with your fingers or a burnisher, and allow it to dry.

Cut a window the size of the brass blank out of the other piece of paper and use it to find and trace the area of the image that you want to use. Cut out the image just inside the pencil lines using a craft knife and ruler. Set it aside. Clean the brass blank with warm water, soap, and steel wool, then pat it dry. Place the trimmed image face down on a protected surface and lightly coat the back with spray adhesive, then adhere it to the brass blank. Let the image dry completely and then seal it with clear polyurethane spray. Let it dry completely, then spray on a second coat. Let it dry.

2 Apply craft adhesive to the back of the blank and press it firmly onto the beading foundation. Let it dry.

3 Thread a needle with an arm's length or more of brown thread and secure it in the back of the foundation. Push your needle through to the top surface anywhere next to the edge of the blank. Using one-bead stitch, sew on 8°s individually around the edge of the blank, with their holes facing outward—don't backstitch them. Pass your needle twice through every bead to secure them and keep them aligned perfectly side by side (figure 1).

figure 1

4 Make inside picots as follows. Bring your needle up through the foundation, just beside the hole at the outer edge of any 8°. Pass your needle through that 8°, working from the exterior to the interior. String on one green 11°, one bronze 11°, and one green 11°. Pass through the next 8° bead and pull up your thread. Pass your needle through the next 8° (figure 2).

figure 2

Repeat to make these picots all around the inside edge of the blank. After the last picot, push your needle through the next complete picot, and the following 8° at the edge. Then go down through the foundation to the back.

5 Bring your needle up through the foundation just outside the hole of any 8° at the outer edge. Using light bronze 15°s and 2-1 backstitch, stitch all around the outside edge. When you return to the start, pass through the first two or three 15°s and then through the foundation to the back (figure 3). Secure your thread in the foundation.

figure 3

6 Trim the foundation close to the beadwork. Thread a needle with an arm's length or more of neutral thread and secure it to the back of the foundation. Bring your needle to the top between the edge of the blank and the inside edge of the round of 8°s. Slip your needle through an 8°, moving toward the outer edge, and string on two olive 15°s, one green 11°, and two olive 15°s to create a picot (figure 4).

figure 4

Insert your needle through the next 8° bead, moving toward the image. Pull up your thread and pass through the next 8°, moving toward the outer edge. Repeat to make these outside picots all around the edge of the blank. Then push your needle to the back of the beadwork and secure the thread firmly in the foundation.

7 If you plan to make the necklace exactly as shown here, stitch jump rings to the back of the foundation, two at the top and two at the bottom. Arrange them equally from left to right, spaced 9 mm apart between their centers and hanging halfway over the edge (figure 5). (If you prefer to use this component as a simple pendant, stitch jump rings to just the top, hanging halfway over the edge.)

figure 5

8 Trim the suede to fit the back of the beadwork exactly and whipstitch it in place with the green thread.

SUPPLIES FOR THE PINECONE COMPONENT

Mottled green 11° seed beads, 4 g

Light bronze size 15° seed beads, 4 g

23 bronze crystal bicones, 3 mm

1.5-mm bronze micro cubes, 2 g

23 transparent brown daggers, 10 mm

4 soldered jump rings, 5 mm

1 piece of beading foundation, 2³/4 x 2³/4 inches (7 x 7 cm)

1 piece of cream synthetic suede, 2³/4 x 2³/4 inches (7 x 7 cm)

1 piece of green synthetic suede, 2³/4 x 2³/4 inches (7 x 7 cm)

Nylon thread:

   Green

   Neutral

1 pinecone, 1¹/4 inches (3.2 cm) long

2 fronds of preserved fern (or pine needles), 1 inch (2.5 cm) long

1 sheet of domed clear plastic candy molds, 1³/4 inches (4.4 cm)*

Clear gloss spray sealant

Craft adhesive

Size 10 needles, beading or sharps

Small, sharp scissors

Newspaper

Craft knife

Toothpick

Small book or other weight

* Make sure the pinecone fits inside.

DIMENSIONS

4¹/2 x 2 inches (11.4 x 5.1 cm)

TECHNIQUES

Bead embroidery (page 123)

Tubular peyote stitch (page 120)

Whipstitch (page 123)

INSTRUCTIONS FOR THE PINECONE COMPONENT

1 Using large stitches, stitch (baste) the foundation and the cream suede together and set them aside. Cover your working surface with newspaper, spray the pinecone with a coat of clear acrylic sealant, and let it dry. Using a craft knife, cut out one candy mold from the sheet.

2 Arrange the fern fronds on the center of the suede side of the basted piece and place the pinecone on top. If you wish, you may use a few dots of craft adhesive to hold the fern and pinecone in place.

With a toothpick, run a thin line of craft adhesive around the edge of the candy mold. Push it gently against the surface of the suede to capture the pinecone and ferns inside. Place the candy mold on a flat surface with a small book or other item on top, applying just enough pressure to keep the mold in contact with the suede while it dries completely.

3 Thread a needle with an arm's length or more of green thread and secure it in the back of the foundation behind the candy mold.

Round 1. Using 2-1 backstitch, attach 11°s all around the edge of the mold (figure 1).

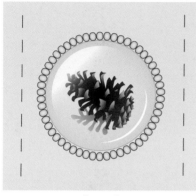

figure 1

Rounds 2, 3, and 4. Working in the base round of 11°s, stitch three rounds of peyote stitch with 11°s. *Note:* Be sure you are working the peyote stitch upward as a tube, not flat as a circular piece. If the number of beads in the base is even, you will be beading the rounds in tubular even-count peyote stitch, and you will need to step up at the end of each round to start the next round.

Round 5. When you add the last 11° in Round 4, pass through the next 11°, string on five 15°s, and pass through the next up 11°. Pull up your thread to see the peak of this pointed picot fall into place. Repeat around the candy mold to make the picots in this final round (figure 2). After going full circle, weave your thread through the peyote stitch, the suede, and the foundation to the back of the work. Secure your thread in the backing. Keep the tail to use for the following steps.

figure 2

Trim the suede and foundation all around the captured candy mold, leaving ½ inch (1.3 cm) of suede and foundation on the edge of the beadwork. Bring your needle through the foundation and suede to the top, just next to the bottom row of beads around the mold. Using one-bead stitch, sew on micro cubes all around the edge, one cube at a time, with the holes facing outward from the mold; then secure the thread in the back (figure 3). Cut the tail and trim the suede and foundation right up to the round of micro cubes, being careful not to cut any stitching.

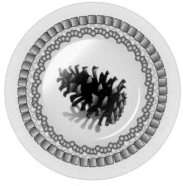

figure 3

Round 6. Thread a needle with 20 inches (50.8 cm) of neutral thread. Consider how the pine-cone is positioned under the mold and mark a tiny dot on the back side of the beadwork to denote the top. With that point representing twelve-o'clock, mark a point at eight-o'clock and secure the end of your thread just to the inside of that dot. Still working at the eight-o'clock point, push the needle to the front, between the

bezel holding the mold and a micro cube. *Note:* On the front, your thread should be in the four-o'clock position. Slip the needle through the cube, toward the outside edge. String on two 11°s and a 15° as a stopper to create fringe. Turn around and, skipping the 15°, pass the needle back through both 11°s and the cube. Pull up your thread. *Note:* You'll be adding the short fringe to the top edge of the component.

Next, push your needle straight down through the foundation; then push it up through the surface just behind the cube to the right. Repeat these short fringes around the upper portion of the dome and down the left side to the eight-o'clock position, as viewed from the front (figure 4). Secure your thread in the back and cut the tail. *Note:* By going down and then back up through the foundation for each individual fringe after passing through a cube, you cause the fringes to stand out crisply at attention. Skipping that step, as time-consuming as it may seem, and simply going directly to the next cube, will cause the fringes to curve backward.

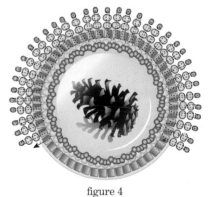

figure 4

4 Add longer fringe as follows, referring to figure 5. Locate the centermost cube at the bottom and secure a new piece of neutral thread, 20 inches (50.8 cm) or longer, on the back of the beadwork behind the cube. Bring your needle to the front and pass through that centermost cube to the outside edge. Count the number of cubes on each side of the centermost cube, not including the ones that have the short fringe. You want to have the same amount on each side; if the quantity isn't equal, fill in any extra ones with short fringe as described in Round 5 of step 3.

figure 5

Central strand. String on thirty-six 11°s, one bicone, three 15°s, one dagger, and three 15°s. Starting with the bicone, pass back through all of the beads on the strand, the cube, and then the foundation to the back. Pull up your thread gently to allow the strand to hang nicely without kinking and to swing gently.

Second strand. You should complete all the strands on one side of the central strand first; then string the ones on the other side.

Pass your needle through to the front and through the next cube either to the left or to the right.

Because seed beads vary in width, even those of the same size, these instructions can't list a specific bead count that gives the desired sloped edge. String on only as many 11°s as you need to make the green section of the second strand short enough that you create an upward slope as you move from the central strand to that second strand. To do so, lay the beadwork flat on your worktable and completely straighten out the first strand. As you string the second strand, push the beads up snugly toward the top of the thread with the tip of your needle until you see the correct slope for the bottom edge of the fringes.

The bottom beads for all fringes are a 3-mm bicone, three 15°s, one dagger, and three more 15°s. For the second strand, add those beads in order when you're sure you have the slope of the 11°s correct.

Remaining strands. Pass through to the front again behind the next cube in line and then go through it. Make the rest of the strands along the same side as the second strand

until you reach the last open cube at either the four- or eight-o'clock position (depending on which side you started). For each strand, make the section containing 11° beads two beads shorter than the previous strand. **Note:** Passing through the foundation each time takes extra time, but the fringe hangs better if you do.

Add strands to the other side of the central strand, using the same bead counts as for corresponding strands on the first side. Secure your thread in the back and cut the tail.

5 Orient the beadwork so that the back faces you. From the top center mark that you made in Round 5 of step 3, measure and draw a dot 4 mm to the right. Measure 10 mm to the right of this dot and draw a dot there as well. Repeat for the left side. Stitch soldered jump rings along the top edge of the back of the foundation, as shown in figure 6, with about a third to a half of the ring hanging off the edge of the foundation.

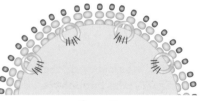

figure 6

6 Rough-cut a piece of green synthetic backing suede that is 1/8 inch (3 mm) larger than the foundation. Place a few dots of craft adhesive on the center back of the foundation. Press the suede gently on top of the glue and let it dry. Trim the edge of the suede to match the edge of the foundation. Thread your needle with 16 inches (40.6 cm) of green thread. Fold back an edge of the green suede and secure your thread in the back of the foundation, anywhere close to an edge. Whipstitch the three layers together with tiny stitches. Secure your thread and cut the tail.

SUPPLIES FOR THE PORCELAIN FRAGMENT COMPONENT

Matte brown size 8° seed beads,
   2 g

Size 11° seed beads:
   Mottled green, 3 g
   Light bronze, 1 g

Bronze size 15° seed beads, 2 g

26 bronze crystal bicones, 3 mm

4 soldered jump rings, 4 mm

Green nylon thread

Crystal FireLine, 1 lb. test

1 piece of broken porcelain,
   1¹/₂ x 1³/₈ inches (3.8 x 3.5 cm)

Cellophane tape

Soap

Fine metal file or hand-held rotary
   tool with porcelain grinding
   disk tip

DIMENSIONS

1¹/₂ x 1³/₄ inches (3.8 x 4.4 cm)

TECHNIQUES

Netting

INSTRUCTIONS FOR THE PORCELAIN FRAGMENT COMPONENT

1 Prepare your piece of broken porcelain by filing or grinding away any sharp edges with the fine metal file or rotary tool. Thoroughly wash it in warm soapy water and pat it dry. Set it aside.

2 Thread your needle with 4 feet (1.2 m) of nylon thread. Using the mottled green 11°s, create a piece of netting as indicated in the following steps and as shown in figure 1.

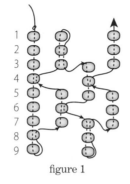

figure 1

Step A. String on one green 11° and tie a single knot around it, then string on eight more green 11°s.

Step B. Reversing direction and skipping over bead 9, pass through bead 8. String on three green 11°s and pass through bead 4. *Note:* Each of the three-bead units that you add in this step forms a picot, and in steps 3 and 4 that follow, you'll use the center bead of these picots to join the edges of the netting to form a tube and to gather the edge of the netting and capture the porcelain fragment.

Step C. String on three green 11°s. Turn the needle around and skip over the last bead and pass through the second one.

Step D. String on three green 11°s and pass through the center bead of the first picot added in step B.

Step E. String on three green 11°s. Turn around and skip over the last bead and pass through the next two beads.

Step F. String three green 11°s and pass through the center bead of the picot added in step D. Continue adding picots, with each row having one at each end and one in the center, until you have the length of netting needed. Create enough netting to surround the piece of broken porcelain, allowing for some stretching to create a nice, snug fit.

3 To weave the two ends of netting together, use the working thread left from stitching the netting and work the needle through the center beads in the picots, as shown in figure 2.

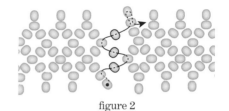

figure 2

4 Place the piece of netting around the outside edge of the porcelain, with your working thread toward the back of the porcelain. Use pieces of cellophane tape to temporarily hold the beadwork in place as you do the following to capture the porcelain in the netting.

String on one 8° and pass your needle through the next center bead of the next picot on the side of the netting adjacent to the back of the component. Repeat all around the edge, drawing it in as you go and making sure to leave enough netting on the front to surround and capture that side next (figure 3). To draw in the netting at the corners, you won't need to add beads between the picots; go directly through two or three picots to obtain nice, tight turns.

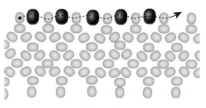

figure 3

Repeat a second thread path all around the component to secure everything.

Work your needle and thread through the netting to the front of the component. Exit an edge bead in a picot. As you did on the back, string one 8° between each center bead of the picots on the edge of the netting on the front side, drawing up the netting as you go. At the corners, go directly through a few picot beads to draw the netting in tightly. Make a second pass through all beads to secure this round. Exit from any 8°.

String on one light bronze 11° and pass through the next 8°. Repeat all around the top edge of the netting. When you return to where you started, pass through one 8° and one bronze 11°; then work your needle through the netting, making three or four half-hitch knots (page 120) as you go to secure the end (figure 4). Cut the tail.

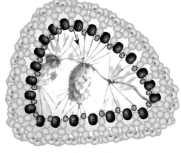

figure 4

Note: To start a new thread at any time, work through a few of the beads of the netting and tie a half-hitch knot around one of the threads in the path. Slip through one or two more beads and repeat. Make about three half-hitch knots to secure your new working thread. End an old thread in the same manner. Snip the tails close to the netting.

5 Start a new thread and work it through the netting to come out at the center of the front of the netting, as follows. Look for the row of beads in the netting that are positioned with the holes facing from front to back, not angled. One row will be closer to the front edge, and that is the row you want. Work your needle to one of those beads and push it through toward you.

String on one bronze 15°, one bicone, and one bronze 15°. Skip over several beads and push your needle through the next bead that resides in the same position in the netting as the bead where you just came out, with the holes facing from front to back (figure 5). Insert the needle through that bead toward you again. Pull up your thread.

figure 5

Repeat adding the trio of beads all around the outside edge of the netting. Remember to always pass your needle *toward* you through the row of netting beads to cause the newly added beads to sit at the same slight angle all the way around the netting. At the end, secure your thread by making several half-hitch knots and cutting the tail.

6 Determine at which beads in the netting you want connection points. You'll need two at the top of the component as well as two at the bottom if you want to make the necklace as shown in these pages (or just two at the top if you're making only this component to wear as a pendant). Thread a needle with FireLine and use it doubled. Work the thread into the netting using half-hitch knots to secure the thread. Bring your needle out of the first bead that you've selected as a connecting point and pass the needle through a jump ring and through the bead just next to where you came out. Work your needle through a few surrounding beads to turn around, which will relieve the stress on the original single bead. Make four more passes through the jump ring, with the turn-arounds in neighboring beads. Travel through the netting following the original thread paths to arrive at the position of the next jump ring. Attach all of your rings in the manner described. When all are attached, secure your thread with half hitches again and cut the tail (figure 6).

figure 6

SUPPLIES FOR ASSEMBLING

10 bronze crystal bicones, 4 mm

Bronze crystal pearls:

    4, 8 mm

    6, 6 mm

    4, 5 mm

    22, 4 mm

8 crimp beads, 2 mm

2 antique brass eye pins, 2 inches (5.1 cm)

18 oval jump rings, 3 x 4 mm

2 tourmaline crystal two-loop connectors, 6 mm

25 to 30 inches (63.5–76.2 cm) of antique brass round link chain, 3 mm

1 antique brass filigree 2-loop clasp

16 inches (40.6 cm) of 49-strand .019 stringing wire

Wire cutter

Crimping tool

Round-nose pliers

Chain-nose pliers

Regular small pliers with ridges (not jewelry pliers)

INSTRUCTIONS FOR ASSEMBLING

Make Connecting Strands and Eye Pins

1 Cut the stringing wire into four pieces, each 10 inches (25.4 cm) long, which allows for about 3 inches (7.6 cm) extra at each end. String four individual strands based on the component to which it will attach.

Note: You may string the beads in a different order than is described here to make your connecting strands.

On all of the strands, string a crimp bead and feed the end of the stringing wire back through the crimp bead. When you start stringing each individual strand, insert the short tail of the stringing wire through the first four to five beads in front of the crimp bead. String the beads according to the guidelines listed below for the strands of the wrapping paper and porcelain components. When all beads are strung, pull up the slack to make a 2-mm loop on the end. Crimp the bead, snip the tail, and set aside the strand.

Wrapping Paper Component, strand 1 (top left). String one bicone, one 8-mm pearl, one 6-mm pearl, one 5-mm pearl, three 4-mm pearls, and one bicone.

Wrapping Paper Component, strand 2 (top right). String one bicone, one 8-mm pearl, one 6-mm pearl, one 5-mm pearl, seven 4-mm pearls, and one bicone.

Porcelain Component, strand 3 (bottom left). String one bicone, one 8-mm pearl, one 6-mm pearl, one 5-mm pearl, five 4-mm pearls, and one bicone.

Porcelain Component, strand 4 (bottom right). String one bicone, one 8-mm pearl, one 6-mm pearl, one 5-mm pearl, seven 4-mm pearls, and one bicone.

2 Add beads to an eye pin by slipping a 6-mm pearl and one bicone onto one of them. Use round-nose and chain-nose pliers to turn a 3-mm loop at the top just above the bicone that matches the loop at the bottom. Repeat for the second eye pin.

Connect the Parts

Connect the components using chain-nose pliers, as follows.

Right side of necklace, bottom of wrapping component. Attach two oval jump rings to the soldered rings on the upper right side of the candy mold and then attach those jump rings to the tourmaline two-loop connectors. Also, attach oval jump rings to the two soldered jump rings at the bottom of the wrapping paper component; then attach them to the top rings of the connectors.

Right side of necklace, top of wrapping paper component. Attach oval jump rings to the two soldered jump rings at the top of the component. With the largest bead at the bottom of Strands 1 and 2, connect the 2-mm loops on the strands to those jump rings (figure 1).

figure 1

Attach oval jump rings at the other end of each strand. To the left strand attach a piece of chain 5⅝ inches (14.3 cm) long. To the right jump ring, attach a piece of chain 5½ inches (14 cm) long. Then use two jump rings to connect the chains' other ends to half of the clasp.

Left side of necklace, bottom of porcelain component. Attach jump rings to the two soldered jump rings at the bottom of the porcelain component. With the smallest beads at the top, attach Strand 3 to the left ring and Strand 4 to the right ring. Attach an oval jump ring to each of the soldered jump rings on the upper left side of the dome. With the largest bead at the bottom of Strands 3 and 4, attach the 2-mm loop at the end of each strand to the oval jump ring attached to the dome.

Left side of necklace, top of porcelain component. At the top of the porcelain component, attach an oval jump ring to each soldered jump ring and then attach the eye pins' bottom loops to the jump rings. Next, after adding oval jump rings to the eye pins' top loops, attach the left jump ring to a 7-inch (17.8 cm) piece of chain and the right jump ring to a piece of chain 6½ inches (16.5 cm) long. Then attach two jump rings to the other half of the clasp.

Green Girl Necklace

A carved bone cabochon with a serene face haloed by luminous pearls. Lucite leaves that glow as light passes through them. The most delicate of chains. Soft green hues. All these elements combine to make a peaceful pendant.

SUPPLIES

Olive matte size 11° seed beads, 3 g

Iridescent green size 15° seed beads, 2 g

6 olive crystal bicones, 4 mm

29 olive crystal bicones, 3 mm

1 olivine crystal pendant drop, 8 x 32 mm

19 light green crystal pearls, 4 mm

2 cream crystal pearls, 8 mm

1 cream crystal pearl, 6 mm

3 olive green Lucite leaves, 16 mm

1 carved bone face cabochon, 1 inch (2.5 cm)

2 silver soldered jump rings, 5 mm

2 silver eye pins, 2 inches (5.1 cm)

2 antique silver decorative stem connectors, 1 1/8 inches (2.8 cm)

17 inches (43.2 cm) of antique silver oval-link chain, 3 x 5 mm

8 antique silver oval jump rings, 2 x 3 mm

1 antique silver snap clasp

1 piece of beading foundation, 2 1/2 x 2 1/2 inches (6.4 x 6.4 cm)

1 piece of light olive synthetic suede, 2 1/4 x 1 3/4 inches (5.7 x 4.4 cm)

Neutral size D nylon thread

Crystal FireLine, 1 lb. test

Craft adhesive

Size 10 needles, beading or sharps

Small, sharp scissors

Toothpick

Wire cutter

Round-nose pliers

Chain-nose pliers

DIMENSIONS

Focal element, 3 1/2 x 1 5/8 inches (8.9 x 4.1 cm)

TECHNIQUES

Backstitch (page 124)

Bead embroidery (page 123)

Flat odd-count peyote stitch (page 121)

INSTRUCTIONS

1 Glue the face cabochon to the upper third of the beading foundation. Let it dry.

2 Thread a needle with an arm's length or more of nylon thread and secure it in the back of the foundation. Push your needle through to the top, next to the edge of the cabochon by the right eye. Using 2-1 backstitch, stitch around the cabochon with 11°s, then push your needle through to the back. Bring the needle back up between the edge of the cabochon and the row of 11°s, just slightly above the right eyebrow.

3 Slip the needle through the bead in the backstitched round next to where you came out of the backing. Using 11°s, peyote stitch the row, going across the forehead to the left eyebrow and ending at the spot that mirrors where you started. Pull up your thread each time. To end up with the crystal bicone point exactly in the center of the bridge of the nose at the end of step 4 you'll need to make sure you have an odd number of beads in this row. Pass your needle down through the foundation, then go back up between the edge of the cabochon and the backstitched round of 11°s near where you ended. Pass your needle through the last 11° added in the peyote stitched row (figure 1).

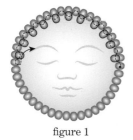

figure 1

4 Follow along with figures 2 and 3. Using 11°s, pick up a bead and pass your needle through the next bead added in the prior peyote stitched row. Continue peyote stitching across the forehead to the opposite side, ending by passing through the first bead added in the first peyote stitched row and down through the foundation. Bring your needle back to the top, passing through the first bead in the first peyote stitched row and the last bead in the second peyote stitched row. Pull up your thread tightly as you go through each row to draw in all of the beads.

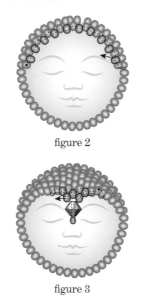

figure 2

figure 3

Continue back and forth across the forehead in peyote stitch in this manner. As you work, tightly pull your thread. With each pass, you'll add fewer beads than in the previous row, until you end up with a single open spot over the bridge of the nose. **Note:** After several rows of peyote stitch, you can weave your thread through the peyote stitched beads to turn around and position the needle to go back in the other direction (instead of going all of the way to the ends of each added row and through the foundation each time). Fill the final open spot in the middle by stringing on one 4-mm bicone and one 15° as a stopper. Pass the needle back through the bicone and weave it through the peyote stitching to one edge of the cabochon; then push your needle through to the back of the foundation.

5 Bring your needle out at the top center of the cabochon, just above and outside of the backstitched round, to begin attaching pearl picots around the outside edge. For each picot, string on one 4-mm pearl and one 15° as a stopper, and pass the needle back through the pearl and the foundation. Pull up your thread and come back to the front surface to the right of the first pearl. Work your way clockwise down the right side, adding nine more picots with pearls, until you reach the four-o'clock position. Repeat on the left side, adding nine more picots with pearls between the top and the eight-o'clock position (figure 4).

figure 4

6 Stitch on two Lucite leaves just under the chin, as follows. Positioning the leaves with their tips pointing up as shown in figure 5 and using nylon thread, bring your needle up through the foundation; then go through the hole in the leaf from back to front.

figure 5

Pass the needle over the edge of the leaf near the hole and down through the foundation to the back; make about five passes to secure the leaf and then bring the needle out of the hole to the top one last time. String on one 15° for a stopper, which covers the hole; then push your needle through the hole and the foundation to the back. Pass the thread to the front again. Using one 3-mm bicone and one 15° for a stopper, stitch on the third leaf, centered and pointing upwards just under the first two.

7 At the base of the backstitched round of 11°s surrounding the cabochon and between each of the pearls, stitch on one 15°, one 3-mm bicone, and one 15° as a stopper. Turn around and skip over the stopper; then pass through the pearl and first 15° and through the foundation. Pull up your thread and bring your needle up between and behind the next two pearls. Repeat all around the face (figure 6).

figure 6

8 Using 2-1 backstitch, stitch around the 4-mm crystal pearls with 15°s, following the contours of the pearls. This stitching will result in a slight scallop. When you get to the opposite side, pass the needle to the back and secure your thread in the foundation.

Trim the foundation closely right next to the backstitched round that you just added (figure 7).

figure 7

9 Thread a needle with an arm's length or more of nylon thread and secure it in the foundation behind the leaves. Push your needle through to the top, just below the center leaf. String on two 15°s, one 3-mm bicone, and one 15° as a stopper. Turn around, skip over the stopper, and pass through the bicone and the rest of the 15°s. Then go through to the back of the foundation. Make five or more of these small fringes on each side of the first one to fill the areas under the central leaf and up to the bottoms of the left and right leaves (figure 8). Secure the thread and cut the tail.

figure 8

10 Trim off the remaining foundation to within 3 mm of the fringes so it isn't visible from the front, cutting about halfway in behind the right and left Lucite leaves. At the top of the component, attach two 5-mm soldered jump rings to the back, using about five or six stitches, placing them 5/8 inch (1.6 cm) apart, and allowing each of the rings to hang halfway over the edge of the foundation (figure 9).

figure 9

11 For this step and the next, refer to figure 10. Thread 20 inches (50.8 cm) of FireLine and use it doubled. Secure it in the back of the foundation, just below the center bottom fringe. String on one 4-mm bicone, one 6-mm pearl, fifteen 15°s, and the pendant drop. You can adjust the number of 15°s if necessary to make the pendant fall nicely with no gaps between the beads. **Note:** The green 15°s will pass through the large drilled hole in the pendant.

Pass back through the pearl, the bicone, and the foundation. Pull up your thread gently to avoid kinking the beads and to allow the dangle to hang and swing gently. Make one tiny stitch through the foundation; then make a second pass through all the beads. Secure your thread in the foundation and cut the tail.

12 Roughly cut the synthetic suede to fit the back of the trimmed foundation. Using a toothpick, place a few dots of craft adhesive at random spots on the back of the foundation, keeping away from the edges. Gently press the suede against the back of the beadwork, smooth it out, and allow it to dry.

Trim closely all around the suede to match the edges of the foundation; then thread 14 inches (35.6 cm) of nylon thread and secure it in the edge of the foundation. Whipstitch completely around the edge of both layers. Secure your thread and cut the tail.

figure 10

13 Place one 4-mm bicone, one 8-mm pearl, and one 4-mm bicone onto one of the eye pins. Using chain-nose and round-nose pliers, turn a loop at the top that matches the existing loop at the bottom. Snip off the excess wire. Repeat for the second eye pin.

14 Cut the chain exactly in half. Using chain-nose pliers, assemble the necklace as follows (figure 11).

figure 11

Attach the bottom loop of a stem connector to a jump ring and the jump ring to one of the soldered jump rings at the top of the beadwork.

Attach the top loop of a stem connector to a jump ring and the jump ring to the loop of a prepared eye pin.

Attach the top loop of an eye pin to a jump ring and the jump ring to the end of one piece of chain.

Attach a jump ring to the other end of the chain and the jump ring to one half of the snap clasp.

Repeat to assemble the chain on the other side.

A

B

C

A Diane Hyde
Ladybird, 2012
17.8 x 22.9 x 8.9 cm
Fabric body, polyester stuffing, Swarovski glass pearls, crystal bicone beads, crystal AB drops, seed beads, frosted Lucite flowers and leaves, ceramic face, leather, feathers, thread, brass rod, wire; bead embroidery, fringing, sewing, wire work
Photo by artist

B Diane Hyde
Scootah Gyrl, 2013
12.7 x 17.8 x 5.1 cm
Fabric, leather, polyester stuffing, vintage porcelain doll head, seed beads, crystal bicone beads and pendants, ceramic face cabochon, watch parts, caster wheel, brass rod, wood base with terra cotta bricks, feathers, wire, brass tubes, typewriter key, brass stampings; sewing, bead embroidery, fringe, wire work
Photo by artist

C Diane Hyde
Halloween Charm Necklace (detail), 2013
66 cm long; largest charm, 5.7 cm
Seed beads, crystal bicone beads, pearls, charms, stampings, vintage key, vintage dice, vintage thimble, vintage watch parts, felt balls, accent beads, Lucite flowers and leaves, scrapbooking items, rubber baby, buttons, guitar pick, chain, clasp, jump rings; bead embroidery, peyote stitch, fringe, right angle weave netting
Photo by artist

Amy Katz

Photo by Betsy Gates

Amy Katz has been part of the world of seed beads since 1993 as a student, teacher, and designer. Her admiration for high-end jewelry serves as her inspiration. Several years ago, when she began designing her own beadwork, Amy made the decision to give it a fine jewelry look by using metal-colored seed beads and such fine materials as crystals and pearls. This has become her signature style. Amy teaches classes nationally and is the co-author of *Beading Across America*. Her book *Seed Bead Chic* published in 2014. You can contact her at amy@beadjourney.com, or visit her website at www.beadjourney.com.

Ocean Memories Necklace

Pearls, starfish, seaglass—you'll re-experience that favorite trip to the beach every time you wear this necklace! The links look substantial and weighty but are actually as light as a sea-side breeze.

SUPPLIES

Silver size 11° round seed beads,
4 g

Silver size 11° Delicas, 10 g

Silver size 15° seed beads, 4 g

34 clear AB crystal rose
montées, 6 mm

2 white round crystal pearls,
3 mm

90–100 clear AB round crystals,
2 mm

8 sea-glass chips, 6 x 10 mm

2 flat sea-glass pendants,
15 x 22 mm

1 starfish pendant with bail

3 elongated irregular pearls,
15 mm

6 crystal-encrusted pearl beads,
8 to 10 mm

2 coin pearls, 8 to 12 mm

FireLine, 6 lb. test

Size 12 needles, beading or
sharps

Small, sharp scissors

DIMENSIONS

18 inches (45.7 cm)

TECHNIQUES

Flat and tubular even-count
peyote stitch (page 120)

Square stitch (page 123)

Flat right angle weave (RAW)
(page 121)

Stitch in the ditch

INSTRUCTIONS

Make Rings for the Central Chain

1 Thread the needle with one and one half arm lengths of FireLine. Leaving a 6-inch (15.2 cm) tail, pick up 32 Delicas and pass the needle through the first three strung to make the ring.

2 Stitch five rows of even-count tubular peyote stitch with Delicas, stepping up at the end of each row.

3 Move the needle down one Delica on the diagonal in the base. Stitch in each ditch in the row with one 15° (figure 1).

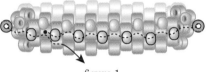

figure 1

For a second row of stitch in the ditch, move down one Delica diagonally in the base and stitch in each ditch in the row with one 15° (again, figure 1).

For a third row of stitch in the ditch, move the needle down one Delica on the diagonal in the base. Tie a half-hitch knot (page 120). Stitch in the first ditch with one 15°. Stitch in the next ditch with one 2-mm round crystal. Alternate the pattern until the row is completed. Weave in the working thread, tie half-hitch knots, and cut the thread (figure 2).

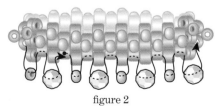

figure 2

4 Repeat steps 1 to 3 twelve more times, for a total of 13 rings.

Make Rose Montée Connectors

5 Thread the needle with one arm length of FireLine. Leaving a 6-inch (15.2 cm) tail, pick up two Delicas. Square-stitch a strip of Delicas that is two beads wide and eight rows long.

6 Note how rose montées have two channels for thread on the back. Pick up one rose montée by passing the needle through one channel and then pick up two Delicas and pass the needle through the other channel (figure 3). Stitch through the last two Delicas in the original strip, go back through the first channel, and pass through the two Delicas that you just added (figure 4). Pass the thread through this connection one more time to reinforce it.

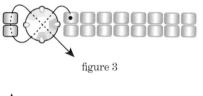

figure 3

figure 4

7 Square-stitch eight more rows and then pick up one rose montée, making sure it faces the same way as the one that you picked up in the previous step. Repeat step 6 to add this second rose montée, but don't add two Delicas on the open side (figure 5).

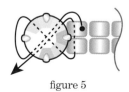

figure 5

Pass the thread through this connection one more time to reinforce it. Make 12 connectors total. Leave the working thread in place.

8 To join the rings to create a chain, pick up two rings and pass the connector through both of them. With the working thread coming out of one channel of the montée on the strip's end, pass the needle through the beads at the start of the square stitch; then pass the needle back through the other channel on the rose montée (figure 6). Pass the thread through this connection once more to reinforce it. Weave in the thread, tying several half-hitch knots as you go, and cut the thread.

Note: When you've completed joining all the rings with connectors, you should have one ring on each end of the chain and a connector in the middle holding two rings in place.

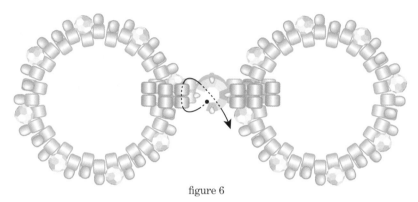

figure 6

Make RAW Chain

9 Thread the needle with one and a half arm lengths of FireLine. Leaving a 6-inch (15.2 cm) tail, pick up eight round 11°s and pass the needle back through all the round 11°s and through the first six round 11°s in the ring again. Using two round 11°s on each side of each unit, stitch in flat RAW until you have a chain 4 inches (10.2 cm) long, or any other desired length. **Note:** You can alter the length of the necklace by making this chain longer or shorter.

Repeat the instructions above to make a second strap of RAW the same length as the first.

10 Pass the RAW chains through the embellished rings on each of the chain's ends. Join the two units on the ends of each chain using RAW (figure 7). Don't cut the working thread; you'll use it later to attach the clasp to the rings if you're short on thread.

Make the Clasp

This consists of two halves: the circle clasp and the toggle.

CIRCLE CLASP

11 Thread the needle with one and a half arm lengths of FireLine. Leaving a 6-inch (15.2 cm) tail, pick up 28 Delicas and pass the needle through the first three beads to make a ring.

figure 7

12 Stitch even-count tubular peyote for five rows, using Delicas. Don't forget that the first two rows make three rows. Step up at the end of each row. Thread the tail, weave it in, tie half-hitch knots, and cut it.

Move the needle down one Delica bead on the diagonal in the base. Stitch in each ditch in the row with one round 11°. Repeat two more times for the remaining rows of ditches.

13 Follow along with figure 8. Place the remaining thread between two 11°s in the center row of ditches Pick up five round 11°s.

figure 8

Put the needle through two round 11°s at the center of the RAW chain. Pick up five round 11°s. Put the needle through two round 11°s on the circle clasp. Reinforce it several times. Weave in the thread, tie half-hitch knots, and cut it.

TOGGLE

14 Thread the needle with one arm length of FireLine and put a stop bead on the end. Leaving a 6-inch (15.2 cm) tail, string on 18 Delicas and stitch in even-count flat peyote for a total of 12 rows. Weave the thread to the opposite side of the piece and position it through an *up* bead (one that's protruding) in the peyote stitch. Thread the tail, weave it through the beads, tie a half-hitch knot, and cut it.

15 Using the working thread, zip the long edges of the peyote stitch together to form a tube. Reinforce the last zip stitch by running the thread through it several times.

16 With the thread coming out of one Delica on the tube's end, pick up one 15°, one 3-mm pearl, and one 15°, and pass the thread through a Delica on the opposite edge on the same side. Pass through all the beads again to reinforce them. Weave the needle through the peyote stitch to the tube's opposite end and repeat to embellish that end (figure 9).

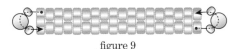

figure 9

17 Center the thread in the middle of the toggle, coming out on the outside of one of the center two Delicas in one row of peyote stitch, and pick up five 11°s. Put the needle through a middle row of RAW in the chain as you did for the circle clasp. Pick up five 11°s. Put the needle through the two designated Delicas in the toggle, passing through the other center Delica from its outside edge. Reinforce the thread path several times. Weave in the thread, tie half-hitch knots, and cut it (figure 10).

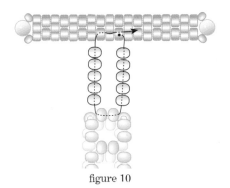

figure 10

Make Decorative Elements

FOR ALL ELEMENTS

As you work, always make sure that the project is facing forward.

18 Using one and a half arm lengths of thread for each element, make five more connectors that you will use to attach the larger beads to the necklace as dangles. To do so, repeat steps 5 to 7 but bead six rows of square stitch between each rose montée instead of eight. Weave in the tail, tie a half-hitch knot, and cut it. Keep the working thread in place.

19 Counting the rings in the central chain, and starting with the first one on one side next to the RAW chain, attach one connector to each of the following rings: the third, the fifth, the seventh, the ninth, and the 11th. Attach the connector in the same manner as you attached the rings in step 8 but attach them around the bottom of one ring only. Keep the working thread in place. ***Note:*** Make sure that all of the connectors are on the bottom of the rings.

ELONGATED PEARLS

This element attaches to the seventh ring using the connector; it is the ring at the center of the necklace.

20 Weave the thread through the beads on one connector to secure it and position the needle in the row of the connector's square stitch that is two rows away from one of the rose montées. Pass the needle to the middle of the next row of square stitch.

Pearl 1. Pick up eighteen 15°s, one elongated pearl, and one 15° stopper. Pass the needle back through the elongated pearl and all the 15°s and to the opposite side of the square stitch in that row. Pass the needle to the middle of the next row of square stitch.

Pearl 2. Repeat the instructions for Pearl 1 but pick up twelve 15°s instead of 18.

Pearl 3. Repeat the instructions for Pearl 1, but pick up six 15°s instead of 18. Then weave in the thread, tying several half-hitch knots as you go, and cut it.

STARFISH

Thread 18 inches (45.7 cm) of thread. Leaving a 6-inch (15.2 cm) tail, pick up four 15°s and stitch 11 units of RAW using 15°s with two beads on each side of each unit. Pass the RAW strip through the starfish's bail and through the square-stitch connector. Join units 1 and 11 of the strip using RAW to create a 12th unit. Weave in the thread, tie half-hitch knots, and cut it. ***Note:*** You might need to modify this step depending on the bail on your starfish.

CRYSTAL-ENCRUSTED PEARLS AND SEA-GLASS PENDANTS

These two elements attach to the rings on either side of the center one using connectors; the rings are the fifth and ninth rings mentioned on page 57. Complete the following instructions on both sides.

21 On each connector, weave the thread through the beads to secure it and position the needle in the row of the connector's square stitch that is two rows away from one of the rose montées. Put the needle in the middle of the two square stitches.

Crystal-encrusted pearls. Pick up sixteen 15°s, one crystal-encrusted pearl, and one 15° stopper. Pass the needle back through the crystal-encrusted pearl and all the 15°s and to the opposite side of the square stitch in that row. Weave the needle to the middle of the next row of square stitch.

Repeat to add a second crystal-encrusted pearl to the ring. Weave the needle to the middle of the next row of square stitch.

Sea-glass pendants. Pick up eight 15°s, one flat sea-glass pendant, and eight 15°s. Pass the needle through the connector's beads to the opposite side of the square stitch in that row. Weave in the thread, tying several half-hitch knots as you go, and cut it.

SEA-GLASS CHIPS, COIN PEARLS, AND CRYSTAL-ENCRUSTED PEARLS

These elements attach to the rings on either side of the prior two using the connectors; the rings are the third and eleventh rings mentioned earlier. Do the following on both sides.

On each connector, weave the thread through the beads to secure it and position the needle in the row of the connector's square stitch that is two rows away from one of the rose montées. Put the needle in the middle of the two square stitches.

Sea-glass chips. Pick up two 15°s, one sea-glass chip, two 15°s, one sea-glass chip, two 15°s, one sea-glass chip, two 15°s, one sea-glass chip, and one 15° stopper. Take the needle back through the bottom sea-glass chip and all the beads above it. Pass the needle through the beads to the opposite side of the square stitch in that row. Weave the needle to the middle of the next row of square stitch.

Coin pearls. Pick up 16 size 15°s, one coin pearl, and one 15° stopper. Pass the needle back through the coin pearl and the sixteen 15°s. Pass the needle through the beads to the opposite side of the square stitch in that row. Weave the needle to the middle of the next row of square stitch.

Crystal-encrusted pearls. Pick up 20 size 15°s, one crystal-encrusted pearl, and one 15° stopper. Take the needle back through the crystal-encrusted pearl and the twenty 15°s and to the opposite side of the square stitch in that row. Weave in the thread, tying several half-hitch knots as you go, and cut it.

SUPPLIES

14-karat gold size 11° round seed beads, 8–12 g*

Gold-plated size 11° Delicas, 2–4 g*

Gold size 15° seed beads, 0.5–1.5 g

Ammolite or other cabochon, 1½ x ⅝ inches (3.8 x 1.6 cm)

42 faceted black agate beads, 2 mm

Beading foundation, 2 x 1⅛ inches (5.1 x 2.8 cm)

1 piece of black synthetic suede, 2 x 1⅛ inches (5.1 x 2.8 cm)

FireLine, 6 lb. test

Craft adhesive

Size 12 needles, beading or sharps

Small, sharp scissors

* A longer bracelet will require a larger quantity

DIMENSIONS

7 inches (17.8 cm) long

TECHNIQUES

Flat right angle weave (RAW) (page 121)

Bead embroidery (page 123)

Backstitch (page 124)

Stitch in the ditch (page 121)

Flat and tubular even-count peyote stitch (page 120)

Embellishing

Square stitch (page 123)

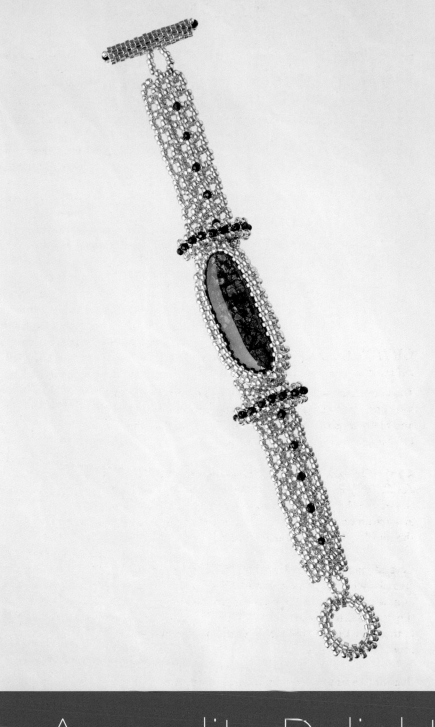

Ammolite Delight Bracelet

Showcase a spectacular cabochon in a chunky gold band punctuated with jet-colored beads. This piece takes its cues from men's ID bracelets, but made in seed beads and accented with sparkling faceted agates, it's completely feminine.

Make the Band

1 Thread the needle with one and a half arm lengths of FireLine. Leaving a 6-inch (15.2 cm) tail, pick up eight round 11°s to create the first RAW unit. Pass the needle through the first four 11°s again to place the thread at the unit's top (figure 1).

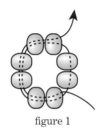

figure 1

2 Still working with the piece of beadwork made in step 1, make a strip of RAW that is five units wide and approximately 1 inch (2.5 cm) shorter than your wrist.

3 Continuing in right angle weave, zip the two long edges of the five rows to make a tube by adding four more beads (two sides) to the first unit and two more beads (one side) to the remaining units, using two round 11°s. Put the needle through the two adjacent round 11°s on the opposite edge, and move the needle through the three other sides of the square. Alternate thread paths as you continue to zip the RAW, as shown in figure 2. Do not cut the working thread. Weave in the tail, tie a half-hitch knot (page 120), and cut it.

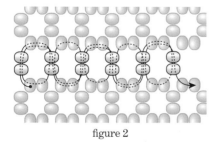

figure 2

Create the Centerpiece

4 Cut the foundation ½ inch (1.3 cm) larger in diameter than the stone. Glue the cabochon to the foundation's center. *Do not trim the foundation.* Let it dry for at least 20 minutes.

5 Bead a bezel around the cabochon as follows. Thread the needle with one and a half arm lengths of FireLine, tie a knot at the end, and pass the needle from the foundation's back to its front, putting the needle next to the cabochon. Using 2-3 backstitch (where you'll pick up two beads and pass through three beads; see page 124), bead around the cabochon until you have an even number of Delicas surrounding it (figure 3).

figure 3

Using the beads in the backstitched row as the base, stitch in even-count tubular peyote stitch, working 4 to 10 rows depending on the cabochon's depth, as shown in figure 4.

figure 4

Because you're working in even-count tubular peyote stitch, you have to step up in every row, passing the thread through the first bead in the current round before starting a new round.

When you reach the bezel's top, stitch one final row of peyote stitch using 15°s (figure 5), but do not step up. **Note:** Using the smaller 15°s causes the bezel's top to pull in and hug the cabochon.

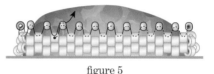

figure 5

6 Stitch in the ditch to embellish the base, as follows. Move the needle down one Delica bead on the diagonal in the bezel. Stitch in each ditch in the row with one round 11°.

Move the needle down diagonally to the bottom row of ditches in the base. Stitch in each ditch in the row with one round 11° (figure 6).

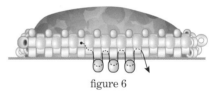

figure 6

7 Glue the piece of synthetic suede to the foundation's back. Let it dry for at least 20 minutes. Cut the suede even with the foundation's edge.

8 Thread the needle with one arm length of FireLine and tie a knot at the end. Poke the needle between the synthetic suede and the foundation; then pass the needle down through the foundation. Pick up one 15°, one round 11°, and one 15°. Sew through the synthetic suede, the foundation, and the last 15° added. Pick up one round 11° and one 15°. Sew through the synthetic suede, the foundation, and the last 15° added, forming a picot. Repeat until you've made picots all the way around the bottom of the stone (figure 7). For the last stitch, put on one round 11° between the two existing 15°s. Then weave the existing thread through two round 11°s in the picot on one side of the stone.

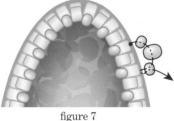

figure 7

9 Pick up two Delicas and square-stitch them together, using the top two designated round 11°s in the picot as the base. Make the square-stitch strap two Delicas wide to fit over the band. Once completed, weave the strap to two 11°s in the picot on the opposite end of the stone (figures 8 and 9).

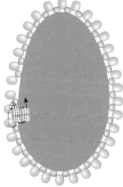

figure 8

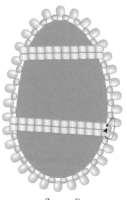

figure 9

Make a second strap on the cabochon's other end, adding thread if necessary.

Make the Embellished Rings

10 Thread the needle with one arm length of FireLine. Leaving a 6-inch (15.2 cm) tail, string on 30 Delicas. Run the needle back through the first three Delicas strung to make a ring.

11 Using Delicas, stitch in even-count tubular peyote stitch for a total of five rows. Weave in the tail, tie a half-hitch knot, and cut it.

12 Go back to the working thread. Moving the needle down one cylinder, bead on the diagonal to position the needle in the first row of ditches. Stitch in each ditch in the row with a round 11°.

Move the needle down one Delica bead on the diagonal in the base. Tie a half-hitch knot. Stitch in each ditch with one 2-mm agate.

Move the needle down one Delica bead on the diagonal in the base. Position the needle in the first row of ditches. Stitch in each ditch in the row with a round 11°. Weave in the thread and tie half-hitch knots but do not cut it. You'll use the thread later to tack the circles onto the RAW band.

13 Repeat steps 10 to 12 to make a second embellished ring.

Assemble the Components

14 Slide the centerpiece through the straps to place it in the middle of the band.

15 Place an embellished ring on both sides of the centerpiece, approximately one RAW unit away from it. Using the thread that you left on the rings, tack down each ring by sewing through the beads of the RAW several times (figure 10). Weave in the thread, tying several half-hitch knots as you go, and cut it.

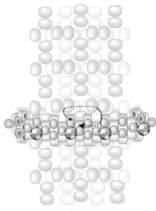

figure 10

Create the Clasp

This consists of two halves: the toggle and the circle clasp.

TOGGLE

16 Thread the needle with one arm length of FireLine. Leaving a 6-inch (15.2 cm) tail and adding on a stop bead if desired, string 18 Delicas and stitch in even-count flat peyote stitch for a total of 12 rows. (Remember, the first two rows make three rows.) Weave the thread to the opposite side of the piece and position it through an *up* bead. Weave the tail through the beads, tie a half-hitch knot, and cut the thread.

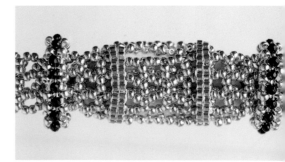

17 Using the working thread, zip the two ends of the peyote stitch together to create a tube. When you reach the end, reinforce the last stitch by running the thread through it several times.

18 Using the working thread that is coming out of one Delica on the tube's end, pick up one 15°, one agate, and one 15°. Sew it to the opposite side of the end to cover the opening. Weave the needle through the peyote stitch to the opposite end and repeat (figure 11).

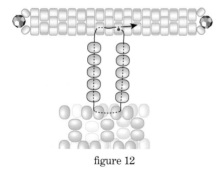

figure 11

19 Center the thread in the middle of the toggle between two Delicas. Pick up five round 11°s and put the needle through the two innermost beads in the middle two rows on the RAW band's short edge. Pick up five round 11°s. Put the needle through the two designated Delicas in the toggle (figure 12). Pass the thread through all the beads in the connection several times to reinforce the stitching. Weave in the thread, tying several half-hitch knots as you go, and cut it.

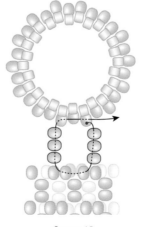

figure 12

CIRCLE CLASP

20 Thread the needle with one and a half arm lengths of FireLine and leave a 6-inch (15.2 cm) tail. Pick up 28 Delicas and pass the needle through the first three beads to make a ring.

21 Using Delicas, stitch in even-count tubular peyote stitch for a total of five rows. Weave the tail through the beads, tie a half-hitch knot, and cut the thread. Embellish the ring as you did in step 12 for the other rings, stitching in the ditch with round 11°s on both edges but also using round 11°s to embellish the center ditch of Delicas.

22 Pass the needle through two round 11°s in the center ditch on the clasp and, using the remaining thread, pick up three round 11°s (figure 13). The circle clasp is attached much like the toggle is. Use the two beads at the band's center that are each part of a RAW unit on the band's short edge. Then pick up three round 11°s and pass the needle through the two designated Delicas in the toggle. Pass the thread through all the beads again several times to reinforce the stitching. Weave in the thread, tie half-hitch knots, and cut off the extra thread.

figure 13

Decorate the Band

23 Thread the needle with 18 inches (45.7 cm) of FireLine. Leaving a 6-inch (15.2 cm) tail, weave the needle into one end of the band, near the clasp. Center the needle in the middle of the two rows of RAW. Pick up one black agate and sew through the two side beads in the third row. Skip a row, pick up one black agate, and sew through the two side beads in the next row. Continue until you've attached five agates. Weave in the thread, tie half-hitch knots, and cut it. Also weave in the tail, tie half-hitch knots, and cut it (figure 14).

Add agates in the same manner to the band on the bracelet's opposite side.

figure 14

GALLERY

A

B

A Amy Katz
Elena's Necklace, 2013
44 cm long
Seed beads, Swarovski pearls, brick
beads, rose montées, round Swarovski
crystals, Swarovski bicones; right angle
weave, square stitch, even-count
tubular peyote stitch
Photo by Carrie Johnson

B Amy Katz
Cordially Yours, 2013
20 cm long
Seed beads, round Swarovski crystals,
tiger's-eye; square stitch, even-count
tubular peyote stitch
Photo by Carrie Johnson

Rachel Nelson-Smith

Photo by Sharif Photography

As a master beadweaver, Rachel Nelson-Smith has taught and shown her work internationally. Examples of her vibrant work appear in numerous publications. She has written two books, *Seed Bead Fusion* and *Rachel Nelson-Smith's Bead Riffs*, and a third is in the works.

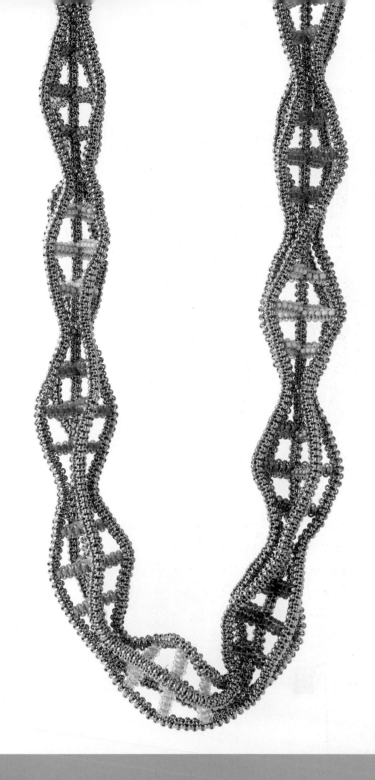

SUPPLIES

11° round seed beads:
- A, bronze metallic, 60 g
- B, matte transparent violet, 5 g
- C, silver metallic, 4 g
- D, matte blue metallic, 5 g
- E, matte transparent
  chartreuse, 5 g
- F, matte transparent fuchsia, 5 g
- G, matte transparent aqua, 5 g
- H, semi-matte opaque
  olivine, 5 g

Gold nylon thread

Size 12 beading needles

Small, sharp scissors or
  thread cutter

DIMENSIONS
36 inches (91.4 cm) long

TECHNIQUES
Tubular even-count peyote stitch
  (page 120)

INSTRUCTIONS
Overview

The necklace consists of a core
surrounded by four spines running
along it. The core and spines are
connected by spokes of different
lengths, which cause the spines to
look as if they're undulating. All
rounds in the core, the spines, and
the spokes use tubular even-count
peyote stitch.

Note: Always bead in the same
direction—clockwise or counter-
clockwise, depending on your pref-
erence. The peyote tube will spiral
in the opposite direction from the
direction that you use to complete
the beadwork.

Since the peyote stitch is tubular
even-count, you'll need to step up
at the end of each round. Each time,

Radiata
Necklace

*Is it a beaded representation of DNA?
Or some kind of a trippy roller coaster?
However you interpret its clever construc-
tion, this long necklace is beading genius.*

pass the thread through the first bead of the round that you just completed before starting a new round. Also, tubular even-count peyote stitching with only two beads in each row requires additional strengthening. To achieve this, reinforce each stitch by repeating the thread path in each round before beginning the next round. The reinforcing stitches are omitted from illustrations for simplicity.

Make the Core

1 The core is made primarily of 11° As, with the other colors strategically placed to aid in the final assembly (figure 1).

figure 1

Rounds 1 and 2: String four As, pass through the first bead strung to create a ring, and tie a knot. The first and third beads become Round 1, and the second and fourth beads become Round 2.

Round 3, odd round: Using As, peyote stitch the round (figure 2).

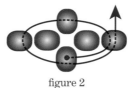

figure 2

Round 4, even round: Using As, peyote stitch the round (figure 3).

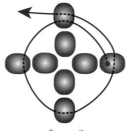

figure 3

PATTERN

After you complete Rounds 1 through 4, complete the following rounds in peyote stitch:

Add two more rounds of two As.
*Add four rounds of two Bs.
Add six rounds of two As.
Add four rounds of two Bs.
Add six rounds of two As.
Add four rounds of two Bs.

Add six rounds of two As.
Add four rounds of two Cs.
Add six rounds of two As.
Add four rounds of two Ds.
Add six rounds of two As.
Add four rounds of two Ds.
Add six rounds of two As.
Add four rounds of two Ds.
Add six rounds of two As.
Add four rounds of two Cs.
Add six rounds of two As.
Add four rounds of two Es.
Add six rounds of two As.
Add four rounds of two Es.
Add six rounds of two As.
Add four rounds of two Es.
Add six rounds of two As.
Add four rounds of two Cs.
Add six rounds of two As.
Add four rounds of two Fs.
Add six rounds of two As.
Add four rounds of two Fs.
Add six rounds of two As.
Add four rounds of two Fs.
Add six rounds of two As.
Add four rounds of two Cs.
Add six rounds of two As.
Add four rounds of two Gs.
Add six rounds of two As.
Add four rounds of two Gs.
Add six rounds of two As.
Add four rounds of two Gs.
Add six rounds of two As.
Add four rounds of two Cs.
Add six rounds of two As.
Add four rounds of two Hs.
Add six rounds of two As.
Add four rounds of two Hs.
Add six rounds of two As.
Add four rounds of two Hs.
Add six rounds of two As.
Add four rounds of two Cs.
Add six rounds of two As.

Repeat from * two more times, weave in the thread, and set the core aside.

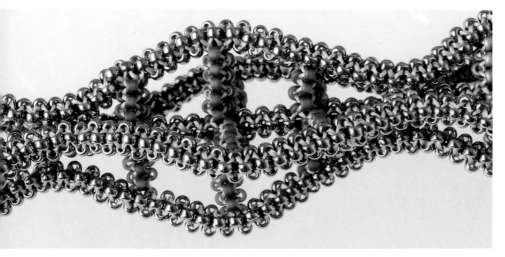

Make the Spines

Notice that the tubular peyote that you've completed had only two beads in each round, but it gives the illusion of having four sides.

2 Following the pattern below and referring to figure 4, work in tubular even-count peyote stitch to create a spine just as you did for the core in step 1. **Note:** You add all beads other than As on one side of the spine.

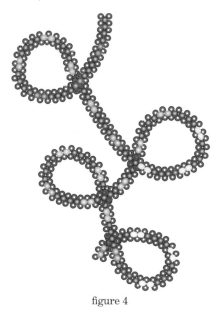

figure 4

PATTERN

The initial circle of 4 As makes the first two rounds.

Add seven more rounds of two As.
*Add one round of one A and one B.
Add one round of two As.
Add one round of one A and one B.
Add nine rounds of two As.
Add one round of one A and one B.
Add one round of two As.
Add one round of one A and one B.
Add nine rounds of two As.
Add one round of one A and one B.
Add one round of two As.
Add one round of one A and one B.
Add nine rounds of two As.
Add one round of one A and one C.
Add one round of two As.
Add one round of one A and one C.
Add nine rounds of two As.
Add one round of one A and one D.
Add one round of two As.
Add one round of one A and one D.
Add nine rounds of two As.
Add one round of one A and one D.
Add one round of two As.
Add one round of one A and one D.
Add nine rounds of two As.
Add one round of one A and one C.
Add one round of two As.
Add one round of one A and one C.
Add nine rounds of two As.
Add one round of one A and one E.
Add one round of two As.
Add one round of one A and one E.
Add nine rounds of two As.
Add one round of one A and one E.
Add one round of two As.
Add one round of one A and one E.
Add nine rounds of two As.
Add one round of one A and one E.
Add one round of two As.
Add one round of one A and one E.
Add nine rounds of two As.
Add one round of one A and one C.
Add one round of two As.
Add one round of one A and one C.
Add nine rounds of two As.
Add one round of one A and one F.
Add one round of two As.
Add one round of one A and one F.
Add nine rounds of two As.
Add one round of one A and one F.
Add one round of two As.
Add one round of one A and one F.

Add nine rounds of two As.
Add one round of one A and one F.
Add one round of two As.
Add one round of one A and one F.
Add nine rounds of two As.
Add one round of one A and one C.
Add one round of two As.
Add one round of one A and one C.
Add nine rounds of two As.
Add one round of one A and one G.
Add one round of two As.
Add one round of one A and one G.
Add nine rounds of two As.
Add one round of one A and one G.
Add one round of two As.
Add one round of one A and one G.
Add nine rounds of two As.
Add one round of one A and one G.
Add one round of two As.
Add one round of one A and one G.
Add nine rounds of two As.
Add one round of one A and one C.
Add one round of two As.
Add one round of one A and one C.
Add nine rounds of two As.
Add one round of one A and one H.
Add one round of two As.
Add one round of one A and one H.
Add nine rounds of two As.
Add one round of one A and one H.
Add one round of two As.
Add one round of one A and one H.
Add nine rounds of two As.
Add one round of one A and one H.
Add one round of two As.
Add one round of one A and one H.
Add nine rounds of two As.
Add one round of one A and one C.
Add one round of two As.
Add one round of one A and one C.
Add nine rounds of two As.

Repeat from * two more times, weave in the thread, and set the spine aside.

3 Repeat step 2 three times to create a total of four identical spines.

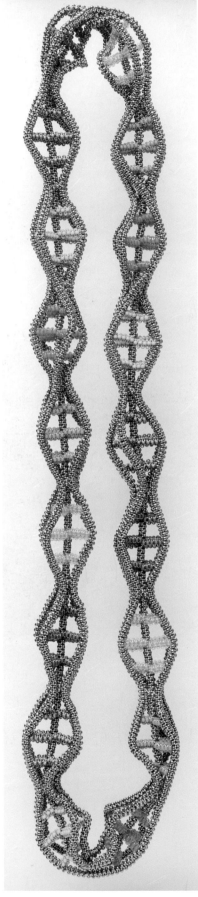

Create the Spokes

The spokes originate from the core, with the end of each spoke connecting to one of the spines. You'll make four spokes of different lengths on the core at each point where the bead color is other than A, and you'll make those spokes in the same color as the ones on the core.

The undulating spines connect to the core by spokes. Within each of the 18 undulations is a set of spokes, all the same color. The middle spokes in each set are nine rounds long, and they're flanked by spokes five rounds long, which in turn are followed by spokes one round long. All spokes one round long are made with Cs.

To begin each spoke, as is shown in figure 5, weave the thread through the beads in the core to exit a non-A bead—the middle set of Bs is shown in the illustration. Work with a single needle and thread.

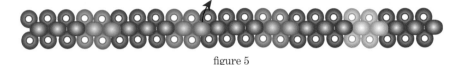

figure 5

4 The instructions in this step tell you how to make one nine-round spoke. *Note:* You attach the spokes to the respective spines as you add them. See step 6 for instructions on attaching each spoke.

Make all 72 of these spokes as are needed along the core, in the central position for spokes of each color. *Note:* When adding up rounds in the spokes, count them on the diagonal.

Round 1: String a bead, and working counter-clockwise, stitch down through a bead in the core that is the same color.

String a bead, and working counter-clockwise, pass up through the core bead where you initially started to complete the round (figure 6).

figure 6

Rounds 2 through 9: Peyote stitch the rounds (figures 7 and 8).

figure 7

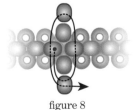

figure 8

5 On either side of the 9-round spokes are 5-round spokes. Begin the 5-round spokes in the same manner as the 9-round spokes but make them only five rounds long. Make all 144 of them as are needed along the core.

Begin the 1-round spoke in the same manner as the 9-round spoke at each set of Cs on the core but make each only one round long. You need 72 along the core; make them all.

6 You attach spokes to a spine as you make them. To attach a spoke, line up one spine with the core so that all sets of non-A beads are coordinated—Bs of the core with Bs of the spine, Cs of the core with Cs of the spine, and so on.

Working in tubular even-count peyote stitch again and without adding new beads, stitch through one coordinating bead on the spine, through the other bead in the last round on the spoke, and through the other co-ordinating bead of the spine (figure 9). Repeat the thread path to secure this attachment. Weave back to the next spot on the core to add the next spoke.

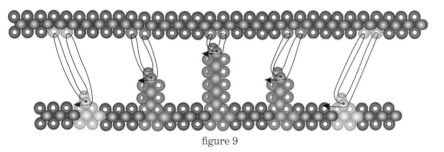

figure 9

Finish the Necklace

7 After you've attached all the spines to the spokes, it is time to connect the two ends of the necklace to form a continuous circle of beadwork, needing no clasp. Working in tubular even-count peyote stitch and without adding new beads, stitch through the coordinating bead at one end of the core and weave as described in step 7 (figure 10). Remember to reinforce this connection.

figure 10

SUPPLIES

11° seed beads:

Dark silver metallic, 58 g
Matte charcoal, 3 g

Gray Silamide thread

Size 12 beading needles

Thread cutter or small,
sharp scissors

DIMENSIONS

8⁵⁄₈ x 1³⁄₄ inches (21.9 x 4.4 cm)

Fits a 7¹⁄₂-inch (19 cm) wrist

TECHNIQUES

Flat right angle weave (RAW)
(page 121)

Tubular even-count
peyote stitch (page 120)

INSTRUCTIONS

Overview

Each of the 18 components starts as a base in RAW, which you work flat and join to form the tube. Each base has loops built off it in tubular even-count peyote stitch. You'll add RAW hooks to one base unit and link the two end components using their loops and hooks in an ingenious way. Work with a single thread.

Loricatus Cuff

In this marvel of bead engineering, looping components made of tubular even-count peyote stitch and right angle weave are joined in a series to create a wide band long enough to span the wrist. One end is then finished with three handmade hook shapes woven out of seed beads. This piece is an impressive and somewhat challenging project.

Create the Components

BASE

1 Weave a flat rectangle of RAW that is 16 units long and three units wide using dark silver 11°s (figure 1). **Note:** As you finish one unit, reinforce it by repeating the thread path before beginning the next unit. This second pass strengthens the beadwork.

2 Continuing in right angle weave, close the three rows into a tube by adding single beads to create a fourth unit that borrows beads from the first and third rows, as shown with the black thread path in figure 2. Finally, close the units on the ends by stitching through the four beads there, as shown with the orange lines in figure 2.

Repeat to make 17 more components.

Loops

3 Working in tubular even-count peyote stitch, you'll add three loops using the base of RAW.

Figure 3 identifies the RAW units where the loops begin and end. Stitch through beads in the base indicated by the sets of dots. Begin the first loop at the yellow dots and connect it to the blue dots. Begin the second loop at the green dots and connect it to the black dots. Begin the third loop at the pink dots and connect it to the purple dots.

Use the set of beads identified with the yellow dots in figure 3 to create the first loop in tubular peyote stitch. Weave your thread through the beads in the base to exit right through the bottom bead in the set of yellow beads. String one dark silver 11° and stitch left through the top-most bead in the same set. String one dark silver 11° and stitch right through the bottom-most bead in the same set again (figure 4). Repeat the thread path without adding new beads. **Note:** In tubular, even-count peyote stitch, at the end of each round always pass the thread through the first bead added in the current round, in this case a dark silver 11° first added, to step up and begin the next round of peyote stitch.

4 String one dark silver 11° and stitch through the second bead that you added in the previous round. String one dark silver 11° and stitch through the first bead that you added in the previous round (figure 5). **Note:** Always repeat the thread path for rounds of peyote stitch without adding new beads to reinforce the stitching before the step-up.

Repeat to add a total of 39 rounds, counting on the diagonal.

5 Attach the 39th round to the base beads indicated by the blue dots in figure 3 as if they were the 40th row, thereby forming a loop.

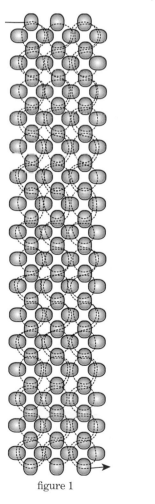

figure 1   figure 2   figure 3

figure 4   figure 5

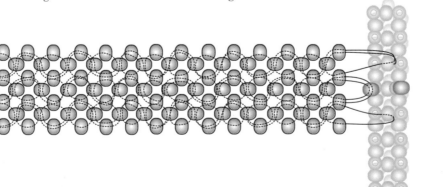

6 Repeat steps 3 to 5 to add 39-round loops to the beads identified with the green to black, and pink to purple dots (figure 6). Set aside this first base with loops.

7 Repeat steps 3 to 6 seventeen more times to add loops to all components created in steps 1 and 2.

Make the Clasp

Add beadwork in the shape of hooks to just one of the completed components on the opposite side of the base from the loops, as follows. (The detail photo at the bottom of page 70 shows what you're making in this section.)

8 Add two dark silver 11°s by stitching through the beads indicated by yellow dots in figure 7. Repeat to add two dark silver 11°s by stitching through the beads indicated by purple dots, and add two more by stitching through the beads indicated by green dots.

9 Work flat RAW that is 15 units long and three units wide up from the two base beads indicated by yellow dots and the left-most bead added in the previous step. Close the flat RAW into a tube as in step 2, incorporating the right-most bead added in the previous step (figure 8).

10 Pass the thread through the beads on the top side in a U-shape without adding new beads (figure 9). Turn around and repeat the thread path to secure the stitching. *Note:* This stitching pulls the beadwork into the hook shape, with the gathered side becoming the inside wall of the hook.

11 Weave your thread through the beads to come out at the first dark silver 11° in the hook that is next to the base, on the outside of the first cube that you added (in other words, the side

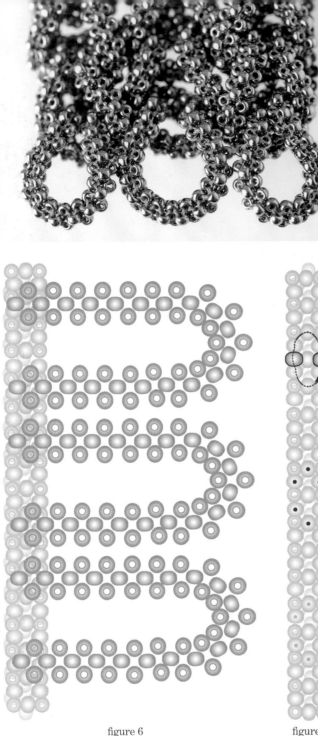

figure 6

figure 7

figure 8

figure 9

on the outside of the curve of the hook). String on one dark silver 11° and pass your thread through the next bead on the outside edge of the hook. Continue adding one bead between each unit along that edge of the hook and up the other side (figure 10). Turn around and repeat your thread path to secure the beading. These beads will expand the outside edge of the hook.

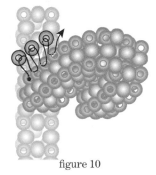

figure 10

12 Repeat steps 8 to 11 to add two more hooks, one at the blue dots and one at the green dots shown in figure 7.

Link the Components

13 String the three loops of one of the 18 components that you made in steps 1 to 8 through the loops of the clasp. In turn, string the three loops of another of the 18 components through the corresponding loops of the first component that you added, and so on, until you've incorporated all the components.

14 Secure the final linked component by stitching its

loops together, as shown with the black lines of the thread path in figure 11.

Bind the Edges

Add short lengths of tubular even-count peyote stitch to the outer edges of the bracelet, between the base of one component and the next. Only two bindings extend from the base of the clasp to the base of the first component and from the base of the second-to-last component back to the base of the final component. Four bindings extend from all other components' bases.

15 Weave your thread through the beads to exit the unit at the interior of the RAW tube that forms the base of the clasp. Add two matte charcoal 11°s as you did in figure 4 (figure 12). Reinforce the beads and step up.

16 Using two matte charcoal 11°s in each row, add four more rows of tubular peyote stitch as shown in figure 5. Connect this length of peyote to the first inside RAW unit of the base of the next component as though it were a sixth row (figure 13).

17 Connect all bases of the remaining components along both edges as described in steps 15 and 16.

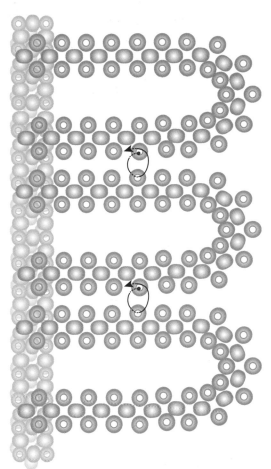

figure 11

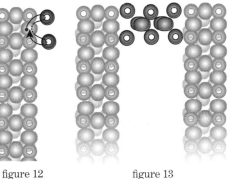

figure 12   figure 13

A Rachel Nelson-Smith
Bursting at the Dreams: A Collaboration with Patty Lakinsmith, 2012
50 x 35 x 4 cm
Handmade brass-riveted, stamped, and capped glass beads by Patty Lakinsmith, glass beads, U.S. currency, resin, nylon; peyote stitch, right angle weave
Photo by artist

B Rachel Nelson-Smith
Beon Freo, 2012
30 x 30 cm
Glass beads, crystal beads, plastic beads, sterling silver, nylon; peyote stitch, right angle weave, herringbone weave
Photo by artist

Glenda Paunonen & Liisa Turunen

Photo by Michael Harvey Photography

Sparked by a pair of earrings she spotted in a department store, Glenda Paunonen embarked on a new hobby—beading. Shortly afterward, in 1990, she opened a small bead shop; today that retail store, Beads Gone Wild, has grown into a glistening oasis of creativity. Glenda, known as "The Bead Goddess," is the creative director and heads up the education department at the store, which is called Crystal Creations Bead Institute and located in West Palm Beach, Florida. Liisa Turunen, Glenda's daughter, started beading when she was 14. After earning a degree in Registered Nursing in Finland, she started beading again in 2006. While working both independently and side by side, they co-create with an energy that thrives on diversity, tension, sharing, and collaboration. Between them, Glenda and Liisa possess a broad range of skills and teach more than 100 different classes, from seed beads to wire to metal to fibers. *Beadwork* magazine selected them as one of its Designers of the Year in 2014. Their greatest joy is to inspire and teach others. View more of Liisa's designs at www.LiisaTurunenDesigns.com, and contact Glenda at www.beadsgonewild.com.

Peacock Earrings

The moment you put on these earrings, a new you will subtly manifest itself—slightly more animated, a wee bit more captivating, somewhat more edgy. You'll still be you, only a little more so. You'll want more attention, and you'll get it. Tired of being in the limelight? Just take them off.

INSTRUCTIONS

Embellish with Brick Stitch

1 Thread a needle with a comfortable length of thread. You'll use brick stitch to create rows of beads that are attached to the hammered ring.

Row 1. Pick up one black 11° and push it down the length of thread, leaving an 8-inch (20.3 cm) tail. Hold the bead against the outside edge of the hammered ring, with the hole facing the edge. Pass your needle through the ring and back through the bead from which the working thread is exiting. **Note:** This row is the first row of brick stitch. Make sure you keep tension on the tail when you add the first couple of 11°s to prevent the thread from going through those beads as you work. The place where you position this row of beads will become the earring's bottom.

Repeat adding 11°s in brick stitch until you've added a total of 16 black 11°s on the ring (figure 1). When you have enough rows, you need to secure the tail in the work by weaving the thread through the beadwork and tying a few half-hitch knots (page 120).

figure 1

Row 2. To start the next row of brick stitch, turn your work, pick up two fire-polished beads, and pass your needle around the thread between the second and third 11° on the ring. Pull the thread tight and pass your needle back through the second fire-polished bead added. **Note:** Rows of brick stitch always start with two beads to prevent the thread from showing on the side of the first bead.

Use brick-stitch to bead the rest of the row, each time picking up one fire-polished bead, passing your needle under the next thread, pulling the thread tight, and passing back through the fire-polished bead that you just added (figure 2). Repeat adding fire-polished beads until you have a total of 15 beads.

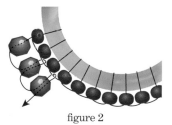

figure 2

Row 3. Now make a third and final row of brick stitch using black 11°s, as follows. Pick up two 11°s and pass your needle under the first thread. Pull on the thread to make the beads fit snugly and pass the thread back up through the second bead (figure 3).

figure 3

Repeat across the row in brick stitch, using one bead at a time to fill the space beneath the prior row, until you have 23 black 11°s (figure 4).

figure 4

Add Rose Montées

2 Weave the thread through the beads to bring it out at the edge of the brick stitch near the hammered ring. Pass your needle under the first thread that lies across the ring. Pick up one rose montée, skip over the next thread across the ring, and pass the thread under the next thread (figure 5). Repeat until you've added eight rose montées.

figure 5

Add Fringe

3 You'll add the longest beaded strand in the middle of the earring and then alternate between beaded strands and chain as you move outward from the center to the right and from the center to the left. Figure 6 shows a schematic; specific instructions follow.

figure 6

Central beaded strand. Weave the thread through the beads and exit at the middle 11° in the bottom row of brick stitch (figure 7).

figure 7

String on two black 11°s, nine blue 11°s, seven purple 11°s, three teal 11°s, 13 dark green 11°s, five light green 11°s, one gold 11°, one pearl, one gold 11°, one bicone, one gold 11°, one drop, and one gold 11° stopper.

Push the beads up against the hammered ring. **Note:** You don't want any thread to show, but you want the beads to hang without kinks in the strand. Skipping over the gold 11° stopper, pass the thread back through all of the other beads and back up through the black 11° that you used on the ring. Weave the thread through the brick stitch to bring it out the first black 11° to the right of the center strand.

First chain, right side. Pick up the last link in one type of chain. Pass the needle back up through the same black 11° that you used in the brick stitch (figure 8). Let the chain hang straight next to the center beaded strand and cut it slightly longer than that strand. (The earrings shown here have 32 links of bright copper chain.) Weave the thread through the next black 11° in the last row of brick stitch. **Note:** As you add them in each consecutive strand, vary the types of chain.

figure 8

First beaded strand, right side. Pick up two black 11°s, eight blue 11°s, six purple 11°s, two teal 11°s, 10 dark green 11°s, five light green 11°s, one gold 11°, one pearl, one gold 11°, one bicone, one gold 11°, one drop, and one gold 11° stopper.

Push the beads up to the ring and, skipping over the stopper, pass the thread back through all of the beads again. Pass the thread into the same black 11° used in the brick stitch. Weave the thread through the beads and go down through the next black 11° on the last row of brick stitch.

Second chain, right side. Pick up the last link in the second type of chain. Pass the needle back up through the same black 11° you used in the brick stitch. Cut the chain to make it slightly longer than the first beaded strand. (The earrings shown here have 29 links of antique brass chain.) Weave the thread through the beads to come out of the next black 11° in the last row of brick stitch.

Second beaded strand, right side. Pick up two black 11°s, seven blue 11°s, six purple 11°s, one teal 11°, seven dark green 11°s, three light green 11°s, one gold 11°, one pearl, one gold 11°, one bicone, one gold 11°, one drop, and one gold 11° stopper. Push the beads up to the ring and, skipping over the stopper, pass the thread back through all the beads again and up into the same black 11° in the brick stitch. Weave down through the next black 11° in the last row of brick stitch.

Third chain, right side. Pick up the last link in the third type of chain. Pass the needle back up through the same black 11°. Cut the chain so that it is slightly longer than the second beaded strand. (The sample has 28 links of antique copper chain.) Weave the thread through the next black 11° in the last row of brick stitch.

Third beaded strand, right side. Pick up two black 11°s, six blue 11°s, six purple 11°s, one teal 11°, three dark green 11°s, two light green 11°s, one gold 11°, one pearl, one gold 11°, one bicone, one gold 11°, one drop, and one gold 11° stopper. Push the beads up to the ring and, skipping over the stopper, pass the thread back through all of the beads again and up into the same black 11° in the brick stitch. Weave the thread down through the next black 11° in the last row of brick stitch.

Fourth chain, right side. Pick up the last link in the fourth type of chain. Pass the needle back up through the same black 11°. Cut the chain so that it's slightly longer than the third beaded strand. (The earrings shown here have 22 links of gunmetal chain.) Weave the thread through the next black 11° in the last row of brick stitch.

Fifth chain, right side. Pick up the last link in the fifth type of chain. Pass the needle back up through the same black 11°. Cut the chain so that it is shorter than the fourth chain. The sample has 13 links—alternating larger links with three small links counted as one—of matte silver chain. Weave the thread through the next black 11° in the last row of brick stitch.

Pearl, right side. Pick up one gold 11°, one pearl, and one gold 11°. Skip over one black 11° in the last row of brick stitch and pass up through the last black 11° on the last row of brick stitch (figure 9).

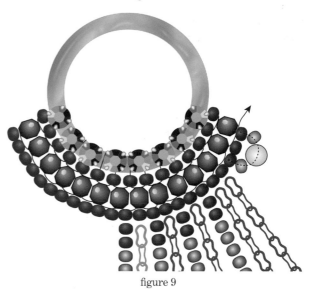

figure 9

Weave the thread through the beads and go through the first black 11° in the brick stitch to the left of the center beaded strand and repeat the beaded strands and chain from center outward on the left side.

Weave in any excess thread through the brick stitch, tie a few half-hitch knots, and trim the thread.

Finish the Earrings

4 Using the chain-nose pliers, attach a jump ring both to the hammered ring at the earring's top and to the ear wire's loop.

5 Repeat all steps to make a second earring.

SUPPLIES

Bronze size 11° Delicas, 2 g

2 blue-gray size 11° seed beads

Gray-blue size 15° seed beads, 1.5 g

2 off-white crystal pearls, 6 mm

2 off-white crystal pearls, 8 mm

1 inch (2.5 cm) of fine sterling silver chain

2 sterling silver ear wires

Gray or blue beading thread*

Size 10 and 12 needles, beading or sharps

Small, sharp scissors

Wire cutter

*Do not use FireLine!

DIMENSIONS

2 inches (5.1 cm) long

TECHNIQUES

Flat circular peyote stitch

Embellishing

Fleur Earrings

Dainty and feminine, these earrings will soon become your go-to for every occasion. They can dress up jeans and a T, yet look equally good with a little black dress.

Make the Large Bottom Flower

Cut 1½ yards (1.4 m) of thread. Using the thread in a single strand, you'll make a piece of flat, circular peyote stitch to create the flower, as follows.

1 Leaving an 8-inch (20.3-cm) tail, string three Delicas and tie them in a ring. **Note:** You want the peyote stitch to lie flat in a circle, not to make a tube. Increases in some rounds help keep the peyote stitch flat. You need to step up at the end of each round by going through the first bead added at the beginning of the round. When you've increased in the first stitch of a round by adding two beads, you go through the bead that is the first bead in a pair of beads only.

Round 1. Stitch around the ring, adding one Delica between each Delica in the three-bead ring (figure 1). **Note:** Since the first stitch of the current round used only one bead, you go through that one bead to step up at the end of the round.

figure 1

Round 2. Peyote stitch around the ring, using two Delicas in each stitch (figure 2). **Note:** You're doing the first step of an increase in this round. Since the first stitch of the current round used two beads, you pass through the first bead in the pair to step up at the end of the round, splitting the two.

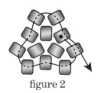

figure 2

Round 3. Peyote stitch around the ring, using one Delica in each stitch, for 6 beads total (figure 3). **Note:** Each time you reach the position where you used two beads in the prior round, you pass through the first of the two beads, add a Delica, and pass through the second bead. You're working the second step for the increases in the prior round, that is, the second step for three increases in total. The other stitches are normal peyote stitch.

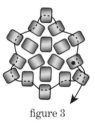

figure 3

Round 4. Peyote stitch around the ring using two Delicas for each stitch, just as you did in Round 2. **Note:** In this round, you're doing the first step of a second round of increases. You should have 12 beads total. Make sure the tail is at the beadwork's back.

Round 5. Peyote stitch around the ring, using one Delica in each stitch, just as you did in Round 3. **Note:** Each time you reach the position where you used two beads in the previous round, you pass through the first of the two beads, add a Delica, and pass through the second bead. You're doing the second step of the second round of increases in this round. The other stitches are normal peyote stitch.

Rounds 6 and 7. Peyote stitch two rounds, using one Delica in each stitch and stepping up at the end of each round. After Round 7, pull tightly on the thread. The beadwork will cup a bit.

Round 8. Peyote stitch another round, using one Delica in each stitch, and step up at the end of the round (figure 4).

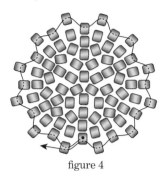

figure 4

2 Weave your thread through the beads to exit at a Delica that is three rounds from the top and stitch in the 8-mm pearl as shown in figure 5. **Note:** It is important to keep the beadwork round, so don't pull too tight. Bring your thread to the outside of the cupped beadwork in that same third round (figure 6).

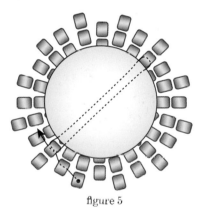

figure 5

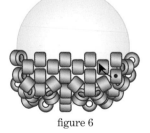

figure 6

3 You'll create rounds of stitch in the ditch by passing through the Delicas on the outside of the cupped beadwork and in the top round, as follows.

Round 1. Stitch in the ditch, using two 15°s in each stitch and passing the thread through the next Delica in the same round (figure 7). At the end of the round, weave the thread through the beads and go back up to one of the Delicas in the top round.

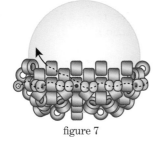

figure 7

Round 2. String three 15°s and, skipping one up bead, go through the second up bead in the peyote stitch (figure 8). Repeat, adding three 15°s around the ring. At the end of the round, weave the thread through the beads to the next up bead on the top round of peyote stitch. **Note:** This bead is the up bead that you skipped at the start of the current step.

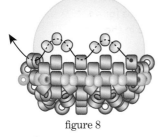

figure 8

Round 3. String five 15°s, skip one up bead in the top round of Delicas, and go into the second up bead, as shown in figure 9.

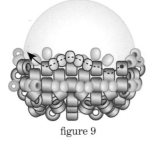

figure 9

Repeat around the ring. **Note:** The current round of 15°s will actually lie under the round of 15°s that you added in Round 2 of this step.

Round 4. String seven 15°s and use the same thread path as you did in Round 3, allowing this round of 15°s to lie between the 15°s in the round you stitched in Round 1 and the 15°s from the round you stitched in Round 3 (figure 10). They should lie snugly between the other rounds of 15°s. Pull out on the center bead to make sure the embellishment makes a nice point.

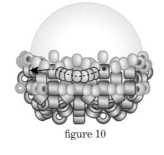

figure 10

4 Using the wire cutter, snip the chain in half, and then in half again. Weave the thread through to exit the center bead of the seven 15°s loop that you just added, then stitch through the chain's last link. Pass the thread through the center bead and the chain's link several times to secure the connection (figure 11). Weave the thread through the beads to the center bead of the next loop in the round and repeat to connect to the second piece of chain.

figure 11

Make the Small Top Flower

5 You'll once again make a piece of flat, circular peyote stitch by stringing three Delicas and tying them in a ring, as follows. **Note:** This flower has a small increase; at times you add two bead in one stitch, but you pass through them as though they're one bead.

Rounds 1 to 4. Using Delicas, repeat Rounds 1 through 4 in step 1, except at the end of Round 4, step up through first two Delicas.

Round 5. Peyote stitch the round, using one Delica in each stitch and passing through two Delicas each time. At the end of the round, step up through the first Delica that you added at the beginning of the round.

Round 6. Peyote stitch the round using two Delicas in each stitch. Step up through the first two Delicas that you added at the beginning of the round.

Round 7. Peyote stitch the round using one Delica in each stitch. At the end of the round, step up through the first Delica that you added at the beginning of the round (figure 12).

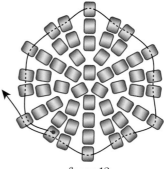

figure 12

6 Pull tightly on the thread to cause the beading to form a cup, and stitch in the 6-mm pearl just as you did with the 8-mm pearl.

7 Make two rounds as follows.

Round 1. Peyote stitch the round, using two 15°s in each stitch. At the end of the round, step up through the first two 15°s that you added at the beginning of the round.

Round 2. Peyote stitch the round, using one 15° in each stitch (figure 13). At the end of the round, step up through the first 15° that you added at the beginning of the round.

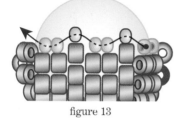

figure 13

8 Stitch two rounds in the ditch as follows.

Round 1. Weave the thread through the beads to reach a Delica in the top round of Delicas below the rounds of 15°s in the cupped beadwork. Stitch in the ditch around the ring, stringing three 15°s each time and passing through the next Delica in the same round each time.

Round 2. Weave the thread through the beads and exit out of the Delica that is one round below the one through which you just passed, that is, the one directly below the current Delica. Stitch around the ring, stringing five 15°s each time and stitching through the next Delica in the same round (figures 14 and 15).

figure 14

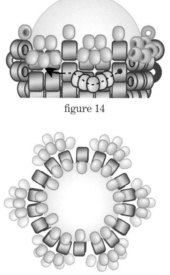

figure 15

9 Attach a loop by exiting an end bead in the five-bead loop. String an 11° and ten 15°s and go back through the 11° (figure 16). Pull tightly on the thread, making the beads sit close together but allowing them to hang well; then pass the thread through the first bead of the next five-bead loop.

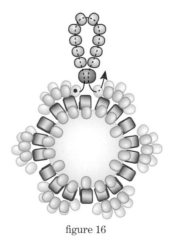

figure 16

10 To give the beadwork stability, weave your thread through the beads to exit at the next bead in the same five-bead loop, moving in the direction of the first loop, and stitch a 15° between that bead and the first bead of the loop (figure 17). Pass the thread through all the beads in the loop two more times to secure the connection.

figure 17

11 Attach the chain at the center beads of the bottom two five-bead loops, as you did on the large flower, making sure both pearls face forward. Then attach an ear wire in the loop.

12 Follow all steps to make a second earring.

Variation

A **Glenda Paunonen & Liisa Turunen**
CZ Cuff, 2008
1.5 cm wide
Seed beads, cubic zirconia rondelles, metal cuff;
herringbone stitch
Photo by Jaani Turunen

B **Glenda Paunonen & Liisa Turunen**
Ravenna Cross, 2012
5 x 3.5 cm
Glass seed beads, glass cylinder beads, Swarovski
crystals, magnetic clasp; peyote stitch
Photo by Jaani Turunen

C Glenda Paunonen & Liisa Turunen
Windows of Sainte-Chapelle, 2012
18 x 3 cm
Swarovski crystals, glass cylinder beads,
magnetic clasp; peyote stitch
Photo by Jaani Turunen

D Glenda Paunonen & Liisa Turunen
Luna Light, 2010
44 cm long
Luna cabochons, crystal bicones;
bead embroidery
Photo by Jaani Turunen

E Glenda Paunonen & Liisa Turunen
Golden Nepal, 2008
18 x 1 cm
Glass cylinder beads, crystals;
peyote stitch
Photo by Jaani Turunen

Sherry Serafini

Sherry Serafini was voted one of the top 10 instructors in the United States by *Bead&Button* magazine's reader poll, and she taught a Master Class at the 2012 Bead&Button Show. She lectures and teaches throughout the U.S. and has won numerous awards for excellence in design. She has written articles for several well-known magazines, and her work has been featured on the covers of trade magazines and catalogs. She is the author of *Sherry Serafini's Sensational Bead Embroidery* and the co-author of *The Art of Bead Embroidery*, which she wrote with her dear friend, the artist Heidi Kummli. Sherry's beaded art is known internationally and is owned and worn by Grammy winner Melissa Etheridge, Steven Tyler of Aerosmith, Lenny Kravitz, and singer Fergie of the Black Eyed Peas. Her beaded artwork is currently being sold through Rockstarfabulous.net.

SUPPLIES

All the supplies listed are approximate. Since every shell will be different, this project is freeform. Feel free to substitute colors to accommodate your own shells.

A, matte golden size 8° seed beads, 3 g

B, bronze size 15° seed beads, 5 g

C, bronze size 11° seed beads, 5 g

D, 300 medium purple crystal bicones, 3 mm

E, 85–100 purple AB round crystals, 2 mm

F, 40–45 copper crystal pearls, 8 mm

G, 50–65 copper crystal pearls, 3 mm

H, 300 cream-colored freshwater pearls, 4 mm

3 seashells, 1/2 to 1 inch (1.3–2.5 cm) at base and 3/4 to 1 inch (1.9–2.5 cm) tall

1 mini sea urchin, 1 1/2 inch (3.8 cm) in diameter and 3/4 inch (1.9 cm) tall

2 split jump rings, 8 mm

1 lobster claw clasp

1 piece of white or gray beading foundation, 5 x 5 inches (12.7 x 12.7 cm)

1 piece of brown synthetic suede, 5 x 5 inches (12.7 x 12.7 cm)

Crystal FireLine, 4 lb. test

Industrial-strength adhesive

White tacky glue

4 beading needles, size 13

Small, sharp scissors

Split-ring pliers

DIMENSIONS

Focal element, 3 1/2 x 5 1/2 inches (8.9 x 14 cm)

TECHNIQUES

Bead embroidery (page 123)

Stacks stitch (page 124)

Standard edge (page 124)

Backstitch (page 124)

Stringing

Shell Shocked Necklace

Seashells and a mini sea urchin provide the perfect focal points for beadwork that is freeform, sculptural, and organic. With that fact in mind, feel free to arrange your shells any way you like and to vary the numbers of the beads in the stacks. Embellish more, or embellish less. Follow your heart!

INSTRUCTIONS

1 Use industrial-strength adhesive to glue the shells and the urchin to the beading foundation, with two shells placed on either side of and slightly higher than the urchin, and one centered below it, leaving ½ inch (1.3 cm) between all elements (figure 1).

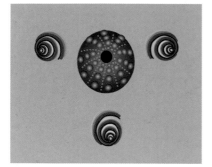

figure 1

Capture the Sea Urchin

2 Thread your needle with 2 yards (1.8 m) of thread and tie a knot at the end. Pass the needle up through the beading foundation and through the hole in the middle of the urchin. String on an F and go back down through the urchin and the foundation. Bring up the needle through the foundation, directly beside the urchin and anywhere along its perimeter. *Pick up one A, six Bs, one C, one D, and one B, forming a stack. Skip over the B and go back down through the entire stack and through the beading foundation (figure 2).

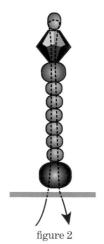

figure 2

Move your needle over ¹⁄₁₆ or ⅛ inch (2 or 3 mm), bring it up through the foundation, and repeat from *. Continue in this manner to surround the urchin with stacks, with all the As in the stack butting right up against each other (figure 3). **Note:** Your urchin may be taller or shorter than mine; add more Bs or use fewer Bs as needed. You want the uppermost B to reach higher than the spot where the curvature of the urchin goes back in toward the top.

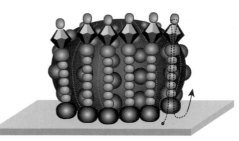

figure 3

3 When you've stitched your last stack in place, weave back up through the first stack and through the B at the top. Pick up one E and pass through the B on the next stack, connecting the Bs. Continue around the entire urchin, attaching the Bs to each other using an E between each one (figure 4). **Note:** You may need to play with the spacing a little! Since sea urchins are not all the same size, you may need to adjust the number of beads by adding an additional E through the Bs.

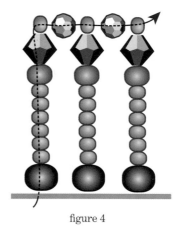

figure 4

Add the Seashell Bezels

4 Repeat steps 2 and 3 around each of the shells. For the tallest stacks, pick up one A, three Bs, one C, one D, and one B (figure 5). **Note:** You may need to accommodate the angle of the shell and make some stacks longer and some shorter. Add additional beads to a stack to make it taller if your shell is higher on one side.

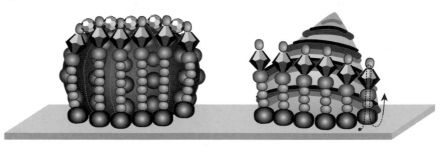

figure 5

Embellish with Bead Embroidery

5 Backstitch using one F at each of the two points at the top that lie between the urchin and the shells and also at each of the two points that lie between the urchin and the bottom shell, as shown for the beads indicated with arrows in figure 6. Using 2-3 backstitch, embroider Hs around the urchin and around the bottom shell, as well as four Hs around the top portion of each of the upper shells. Then continue around the shell with Gs until they meet the Hs around the sea urchin (figure 7). Weave the thread to the underside of the beading foundation and tie it off with an overhand knot (page 120) to secure the thread; then clip it.

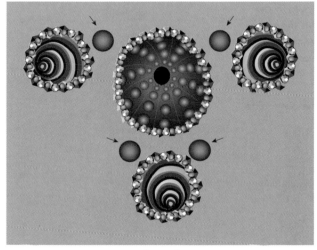

figure 6

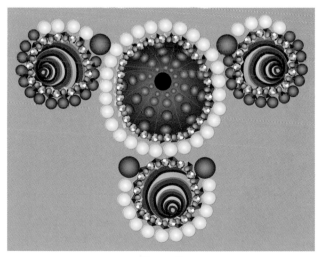

figure 7

6 Cut the excess beading foundation off, making it lie flush against the beads but being careful not to clip any threads.

7 Spread a thin layer of white tacky glue over the back of the beadwork, staying 1/8 inch (3 mm) away from the edges. Press the glued side onto the synthetic suede. After it's completely dry, cut the suede flush with the edge of the beadwork.

8 Thread 18 inches (45.7 cm) of thread and tie a knot at the end. Working with the thread single, make a standard edge stitch around the entire periphery of the beadwork using Cs (figure 8).

figure 8

Create the Neckbands

9 Locate the middle of the beaded piece, which is the center of the middle sea urchin. Measure points that are approximately 2 inches (5.1 cm) from the center to identify the places where you'll begin to make the neckbands. You can mark this spot with a beading needle pushed into the beadwork where the 2 inches (5.1 cm) are indicated.

10 Cut two strands of thread 6 feet (1.8 m) long. Thread a needle on each end of both strands. At one point for starting the neckband on one side, pass the needle on one thread up through one of the Cs. Skip the C directly beside the one exited and pass the other needle up through the next C (figure 9). Do the same on the point for starting the neckband on the other side. Before continuing, hold the beadwork up to your neckline to see if the positioning is pleasing. If not, adjust the placement of the neckbands.

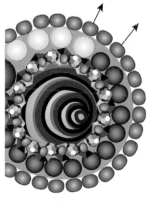

figure 9

11 Working with the thread for the neckband on one side, pick up one H on one needle and two Hs on the other one. With the needle holding the one H, pass through the second H on the opposite thread (figure 10). Alternate the strands, adding one bead to one strand the first time and two beads to it the next time. Repeat this pattern eight times for each neckband.

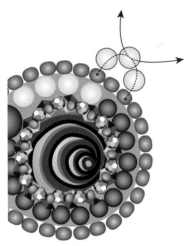

figure 10

12 On each thread, pick up two Cs. Put one needle down and with the other pick up one F, one C, and one F; then continue this pattern for half the length that you want your necklace to be. In other words, both strands combined will give you the total length (figure 11). Pass the other thread up through all the beads just strung. Repeat this pattern for the other neckband.

figure 11

13 Add a split ring to one half of the clasp. Then pick up a split ring with one thread and pass it back through all of the beads in your neckband to move back down to the first C where you started (figure 12). Keep that working thread intact. Pass the other needle and thread through the entire section of the neckband that you completed in step 12, where you used the Fs. When this thread gets to the last H that you added in step 11, pass through it and pick up one C, one E, and one C. Working diagonally, pass the thread through the next H down in the strand. Continue down the entire row of Hs until you reach the first Cs where the other working thread is located (figure 13).

Repeat this step on the other side.

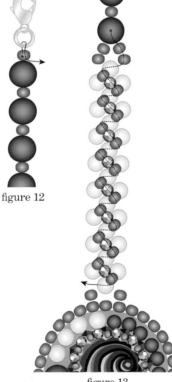

figure 12

figure 13

Embellish

14 Using the working threads, add tiny fringes across the top of the piece, as follows. Weave one of the needles up through an edge C. Pick up one D and one B

and, skipping over the B, pass the thread back through the D and down through the C you first exited. Pass up through the next C and repeat the pattern across the top of the beadwork and down the sides of the piece (figure 14). You've now finished the focal element.

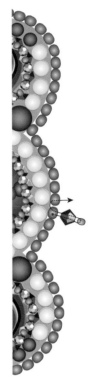

figure 14

TIP

If having four strands of working threads makes you insane, simply weave two of them through the beads, use simple overhand knots to end them, and then work with two strands.

15 Using Fs and Hs and any other leftover pearls you like, string beads onto new thread as desired to create the looped strands that dangle below the focal element. Attach them randomly, working each end in and out of the edge beads at the bottom. Feel free to tangle the strands and attach them asymmetrically as I did to keep the look organic.

SUPPLIES

A, green iridescent size 11° cylinder beads, 2 g

B, bronze size 15° seed beads, 5 g

C, matte turquoise silver-lined size 11° seed beads, 8 g

D, 288 marbled pale green 3-mm magatama drops*

1 marbled blue-green round bead, 6 to 8 mm

4 green crystal bicones, 4 mm

40 to 50 cream-colored glass pearls, 2 mm

15 cream pearls, 4 mm

1 to 3 metal flowers, charms, etc.

1 glass or other type of cabochon, 18 mm

2 glass-pearl cabochons or other type of cabochons, 12 mm

Hook and eye closure

1 piece of black synthetic suede, 3 x 8 inches (7.6 x 20.3 cm)**

1 piece of white or gray beading foundation, 3 x 8 inches (7.6 x 20.3 cm)

Smoke FireLine, 4 lb. test

9 inches (22.9 cm) of green shibori ribbon

Industrial-strength adhesive

White tacky glue

Size 12 needles, beading or sharps

Small, sharp scissors and paper scissors

* The number may vary depending on the size of your wrist.

** Or color to match beadwork

DIMENSIONS

7 x 2 inches (17.8 x 5.1 cm)

TECHNIQUES

Backstitch (page 124)

Bead embroidery (page 123)

Tubular even-count peyote stitch (page 120)

Lazy River Cuff

The elegant flow of silk is the perfect backdrop for a highly embellished bracelet. For this organic, freeform design, use whatever colors appeal to you and any number of embellishment beads that you desire. Sherry chose a calming greenish blue that made her think of a slow-moving river in the summer.

INSTRUCTIONS

1 Photocopy figure 1, which is the pattern for the bracelet. Cut it out, wrap it around your wrist, and decide how tight you'd like it to fit. Allow for 1 inch (2.5 cm) between the ends for the closure. Cut off the ends accordingly.

2 Thread an arm's length of FireLine on your needle and tie a knot at the end. Place the shibori ribbon on the foundation and play with twisting and turning it to determine how you'd like it to lie. It doesn't need to cover all of the foundation, because in a later step you'll hide the foundation by embroidering it with beads. When you like the results, tack all the edges of the ribbon to the foundation, keeping the stitches ¼ inch (6 mm) apart. (You'll attach the ribbon permanently as you add beads.) *Note:* Be careful with your needle when stitching shibori. It's silk, and it can snag!

Bead around the Cabochons

3 Using industrial-strength adhesive, carefully glue down the cabochons any place you like. You can glue them on the foundation or directly to the ribbon but be careful not to let any glue seep out around the edges of the cabochons and onto the ribbon.

4 Thread 1 yard (91.4 cm) of FireLine onto your needle and tie a knot at one end. Working with a single thread and using 2-3 backstitch, stitch an even number of As around the largest cabochon.

5 From the backstitched base row, work peyote stitch around the cabochon to create a bezel (figure 2). Cabs come in different heights. I stitched three rounds of As around mine, but yours may require one more or one less row. The idea is to hug the cabochon. For the final round, use Bs. *Note:* Because you're working in tubular even-count peyote stitch, you'll need to step up at the end of every row; that is, you will need to pass the thread through the first bead in the current row before you can begin the next row.

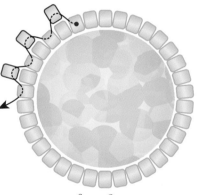

figure 2

figure 1

6 Upon completion of the round of Bs, pass the needle through the A that you stitched on right before you started the final round of Bs. Pick up a C and pass through the next B. Continue stitching in the ditch around the cabochon until you've stitched a C in every space between Bs (figure 3).

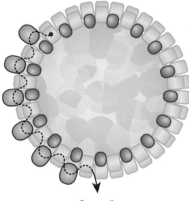

figure 3

7 Weave the thread down through the beads in the bezel to position it on the underside of the beading foundation. Make bezels for the smaller cabochons as you did for the large one.

Add Bead Embroidery

8 Now have fun backstitching! Use either doubled thread in a comfortable length for you or single thread and go through the beads twice. There's no right or wrong place to stitch, and no right or wrong beads to use, but keep in mind where the center of the cuff will be and what you'd like to feature most visibly. Cover all of the foundation with beads. Stitch the beads down one at a time randomly around the cabochons and around the edges of the shibori ribbon.

Pick up a tiny bit of the edge of the shibori ribbon as you stitch down individual beads. Stitch in and around the ribbon, following its curves and stitching a bead where you like it. This project has no rules. Just let go and have fun. Figures 4 and 5 show stitches, such as one-bead and stacks, that you can use.

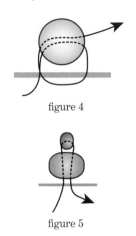

figure 4

figure 5

9 Stitch the hook and the eye very securely to the back of the beading foundation (figure 6). Take special care to make sure the two sides meet properly when clasped!

figure 6

10 Attach the beadwork to the synthetic suede with white glue, keeping the glue ⅛ inch (3 mm) away from the edges so none seeps out. Allow the piece to dry; then cut the foundation and the suede flush against the beadwork.

Add the Edging

11 Thread the needle with a single strand of 1 yard (91.4 cm) of FireLine and knot one end. Sew into the beadwork at the edge to anchor the thread. With the needle exiting the top edge of the cuff, pick up one C, one D, and one C. *Note:* You pick up three beads in this very first step only. Sew down through the beadwork and the suede to attach them. Pull the beads snug. Pass the needle up through the second C strung. The beads will stand up on the edge.

* Pick up one D and one C and pass the needle down through both the foundation and the suede about one bead's width away from the series of beads already stitched onto the edge. Bring the needle back up through the C just strung; pull the beads so that they sit snugly against the edge (figure 7). Repeat from *, working your way around the edge. When you reach the hook and the eye, don't use the drops but keep adding Cs as edging. Resume adding Ds after moving past the closures. When you return to your starting point where the last bead meets the first bead you sewed on, go down through the first bead to attach the two. Pass your needle through some beads on your beaded cuff, making several small knots in the beadwork while hiding them in the beads.

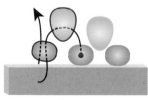

figure 7

A

B

A **Sherry Serafini**
Demon of Screamin'—A Dedication, 2013
46 x 23 cm
Porcelain cabochons by Laura Mears, crystals, pearls, seed beads; bead embroidery
Photos by artist

B **Sherry Serafini**
Monster, 2013
45 x 20 x 5 cm
Glass components by Wayne Robbins, fish leather, crystals, chains, seed beads; bead embroidery
Photo by Larry Sanders

Melissa Grakowsky Shippee

Melissa Grakowsky Shippee teaches beading workshops around the world. She also designs projects for magazines and books, and illustrates project instructions for other beading professionals. Her book, *I Can Herringbone*, released in 2012. Melissa loves studying nature and has always had a passion for science, as well as art. Visit her website at www.mgsdesigns.net, or contact her at grakowsky@gmail.com.

SUPPLIES

Metallic bronze size 11° round seed
beads, 1 g

Size 11° cylinder beads:
- A, matte metallic bronze, 4 g
- B, metallic bronze, 1 g
- C, lined fuchsia, 1 g
- D, matte metallic bronze iris, 1 g

Size 15° seed beads:
- E, metallic bronze, 2 g
- F, matte lined bronze, 2 g

Size 15° cylinder beads:
- G, matte light aqua rainbow, 2 g
- H, matte aqua rainbow, 2 g
- J, light bronze/violet, 2 g
- K, opaque white, 1 g
- L, opaque orchid, 1 g
- M, translucent pink mist rainbow, 1 g
- N, translucent amethyst rainbow, 1 g
- O, translucent light cherry
  rainbow, 1 g
- P, metallic bronze, 1 g
- Q, opaque black, 1 g

4 plum crystal pearls, 4 mm

3-mm metallic bronze magatama
beads, 1 g

Smoke FireLine, 6 lb. test

Size 12 needles, beading or sharps

Size 13 long beading needles

Small, sharp scissors

DIMENSIONS

2³/₄ x 2¹/₈ inches (7 x 5.4 cm)

TECHNIQUES

Tubular even-count peyote stitch
(page 120)

Odd- and even-count flat peyote stitch
(page 120)

Brick stitch (page 122)

Loomwork

Cherry Blossom Loom Pendant

Japanese architecture and arts inspired this pendant. A peyote stitch base becomes the loom off of which to work loom patterns with size 15° cylinder beads. Because of its construction, you can feature a different image on each side—a lovely flower on one, and a kanji meaning "tree" on the other.

INSTRUCTIONS

Overview

First you'll work in tubular peyote stitch to bead a frame, with increases to make the corners, which then gives you the rectangular structure. The frame starts with flat peyote stitch, which then gets zipped on four sides to form a three-dimensional rectangle. You'll then add a bail at the top of the frame. Between the two rounds of 15°s on the edge of each of the two short sides of the pendant, you'll set up warp threads with your working thread, and then use the same thread as you used for your weft threads to add beads to the loom you created.

Create the Frame

Note: Figures in this section show only the first eight beads in each round of the tubular peyote stitch, with some additional illustrations showing the stitching for the corners.

1 Thread two wingspans of single FireLine on your size 12 needle. *Note:* Pull tightly on the thread. You want the beading to be firm. At any time, switch to the size 13 needles if you find that you no longer can get the thread through the beads with the size 12 needles.

Rounds 1 to 3: Pick up 23 As, one E, 41 As, one E, 23 As, one E, 41 As, and one E. Pass your thread through the first two beads that you strung to form a ring, leaving just enough of a tail to weave into the beadwork later and trim. *Note:* The beads that you strung initially become rounds 1 and 2 of the tubular, even-count peyote stitch. The Es in those rounds become the corners of the frame.

For Round 3, peyote stitch with As around the tube (figures 1 and 2). *Note:* For even-count tubular peyote stitch, you need to step up at the end of each round to start a new round; that is, you must pass the thread through the first bead of the current round to start the next round.

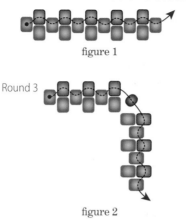

figure 1

Round 3

figure 2

Rounds 4 to 7: Peyote stitch the fourth round with As, adding two As over each E in Round 3. *Note:* You increase over the Es to shape the frame. For Round 5, peyote stitch with Bs, adding one B between the pair of As added at each corner in Round 4. Weave your thread through the beads to the other edge of the strip (Round 1), and for Rounds 6 and 7, peyote stitch two rounds in the same way as you did Rounds 4 and 5 (figures 3 and 4).

figure 3

Round 5

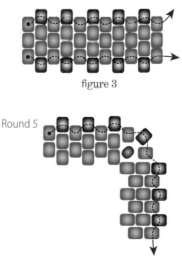

figure 4

Rounds 8 and 9: Passing your thread through the beads in Round 4, stitch one round in the ditch using Fs. *Note:* Pull the thread to make it tight enough to remove all the slack but no tighter. Weave your thread through the beads to Round 6 and stitch one round in the ditch using Fs, just as you did in Round 4 (figure 5).

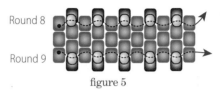

Round 8

Round 9

figure 5

Rounds 10 to 12: Weave your thread through the beads to Round 7 and peyote stitch one round of As, adding one 11° round seed bead on either side of the single B at each corner. For Round 11, peyote stitch one round of Cs, adding one 4-mm pearl at each corner. For Round 12, peyote stitch one round of Ds, adding one magatama on either side of the pearl at each corner (figures 6 and 7).

Round 12
Round 11
Round 10

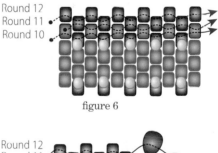

figure 6

Round 12
Round 11
Round 10

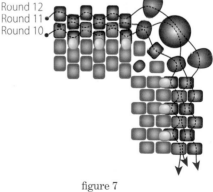

figure 7

Round 13: Weave your thread through the beads to Round 5 and peyote stitch one round of As, adding one 11° round seed bead on either side of the single B at each corner (figures 8 and 9).

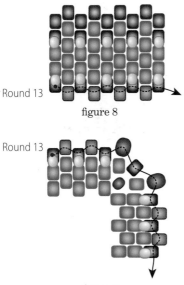

Round 13

figure 8

Round 13

figure 9

2 Zip Round 13 to Round 11 by stitching alternately through the beads in each round. **Note:** Be very careful while you stitch because it's easy to break the As and Cs.

3 Weave your thread through the beads to round 8. Peyote stitch one E between each F in round 8, adding three Bs at each corner. Weave your thread through the beads to round 9, on the other side of the frame, and repeat as for round 8. Weave your tail into the beadwork and trim it.

Make the Bail

4 String 3 arm's lengths of FireLine. Very gingerly, weave the thread through the beads up to round 13, the round of Ds. Bring your thread out of the fifth D on one of the short sides of the frame. Add two As in odd-count flat peyote stitch (figure 10).

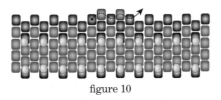

figure 10

5 Reverse direction and add three As in peyote stitch, using an odd-count turn-around (figure 11). **Note:** In odd-count flat peyote stitch, you always end up with an extra bead on the end but have no bead through which you can pass your thread. You need to weave your thread through the beads to end the current row and bring your thread out in the correct place to start the next row.

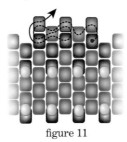

figure 11

6 Continue peyote stitching with As until you have 31 rows.

7 Brick stitch one row of As to the edge of the peyote stitch strip, starting at Row 30 and stopping at Row 2. For the first stitch, pick up two As (figure 12).

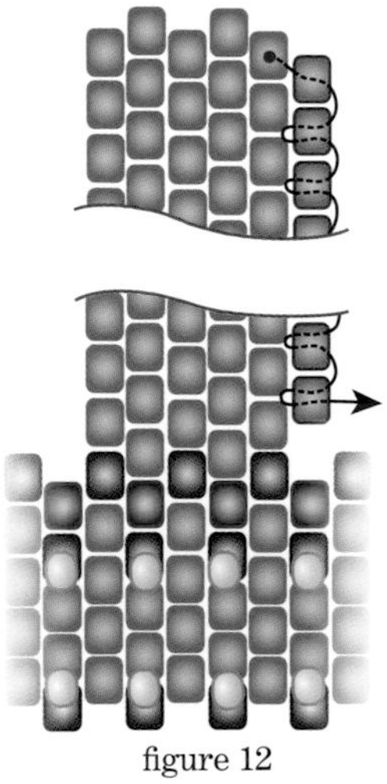

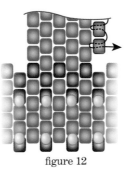

figure 12

8 Brick stitch another row of As on top of the first (figure 13).

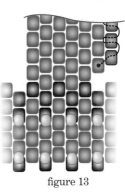

figure 13

9 Repeat the two brick-stitched rows on the other side of the peyote stitch strip to make your bail symmetrical.

10 Zip the last row to the beads in Row 13 that you used to start Row 1.

Loom the Images

11 Set up your warp threads by weaving your thread through the beads to the first F in Row 8 on one of the short sides of the frame. Jump across the space inside the frame to the other short side and stitch through the first E. Jump back across the frame to the first side and stitch through the second F. Repeat across until you've entered the last F, pulling your thread tight as you go.

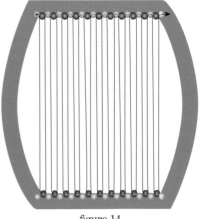

figure 14

The warp threads should be very taut to make the entire frame curve out on each side. Make sure this is happening now, because you won't be able to tighten them after this point (figure 14).

12 Using your size 12 beading needles, loom Side 1 in the center of the frame following the schematic at right. As shown in figure 15, as you loom, bring your row of beads underneath the warp threads; then stitch through the beads with your weft thread on top of the warp threads.

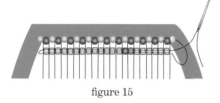

figure 15

13 After you've completed Side 1, weave your thread through the beads in the loomwork and trim it. To prepare to work the second loomed side, thread two arm's lengths of FireLine and weave the thread through to the first F in Round 9 on one of the short sides of your frame. Set up warp threads as you did in step 11.

14 You'll loom the pattern for Side 2 by following the schematic at far right, but for this side you'll work differently than on Side 1. Here, push your row down on top of the warp threads; then stitch through the beads with your weft thread underneath the warp threads (figure 16). When you've finished, secure your thread in the loomwork and trim it.

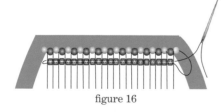

figure 16

To wear the necklace, string the pendant on silk thread or your favorite beaded neck strap.

Side 1   *Side 2*

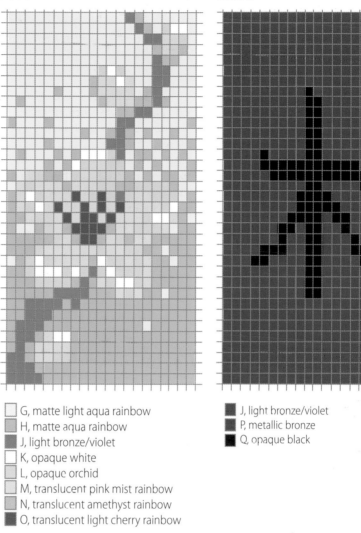

G, matte light aqua rainbow
H, matte aqua rainbow
J, light bronze/violet
K, opaque white
L, opaque orchid
M, translucent pink mist rainbow
N, translucent amethyst rainbow
O, translucent light cherry rainbow

J, light bronze/violet
P, metallic bronze
Q, opaque black

SUPPLIES

Size 11° cylinder beads:

    A, opaque white AB, 1 g

    B, opaque orchid, 1 g

    C, matte translucent amethyst AB, 1 g

    D, matte translucent aqua AB, 1 g

Size 15° seed beads:

    E, ceylon pink, 1 g

    F, matte translucent aqua AB, 1 g

    G, apple-lined jonquil, 1 g

Size 11° seed beads:

    H, matte translucent aqua AB, 1 g

    J, light green lined jonquil rainbow, 5 g

    K, emerald-lined jonquil rainbow, 1 g

2 cream crystal pearls, 2 mm

8 peridot AB glass leaves, 12 x 7 mm

12 inches (30.5 cm) of silver-plated
    22-gauge wire

2 silver-plated ear wires

White size D nylon beading thread

Size 12 beading needles

Small, sharp scissors

Round-nose pliers

Chain-nose pliers

Wire cutter

DIMENSIONS

2³/₈ inches (6 cm) long

TECHNIQUES

Tubular peyote stitch (page 120)

Herringbone stitch

Netting

Morning Glory
Earrings

*These earrings combine a few simple
beadweaving techniques with some
simple wirework for fanciful floral
earrings that are just perfect for a
summery outfit.*

INSTRUCTIONS

Overview

You'll weave the morning glory flower and two sizes of leaves, then create the tendrils by adding beads to some basic wirework, and finally bring all the components together on a fringed base.

Morning Glory

1 Thread your needle with 24 inches (61 cm) of thread.

Rounds 1 and 2: Pick up 10 As and stitch through the first bead again to form a ring. Leave just enough of a tail to weave into the beadwork later and trim.

Round 3: Peyote stitch the round using one A in each stitch; then step up (figure 1). Then stitch through just the beads in Round 3 again, to pull that row together. Then weave your thread through the beads so that it is emerging from Round 1 (figure 2) **Note:** Round 3 should pull the beads together, and your beadwork should take on a cupped shape. Round 3 will be at the bottom of the cup, and you will then work off of Round 1 at the top. Pull tightly to emphasize the cupped shape and your flower will resemble a real morning glory!

figure 1

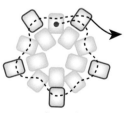

figure 2

Round 4: Peyote stitch the round using two As for each stitch; then step up through the first A in the first pair (figure 3).

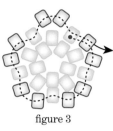

figure 3

Round 5: Add two Bs in herringbone stitch on top of each pair of As from Round 4. At the end of the round, step up through the first B in the first pair (figure 4).

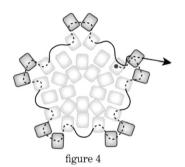

figure 4

Round 6: Add two Cs in herringbone stitch on top of each pair of Bs from Round 5 and peyote stitch two Es between the pairs of Bs. At the end of the round, step up through the first C added (figure 5).

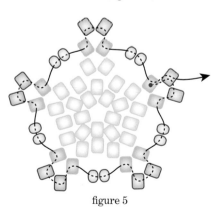

figure 5

Round 7: Add two Ds in herringbone stitch on top of the pair of Cs. Peyote stitch one F, stitching through both Es. Next, peyote stitch one F, stitching through just the first C in the next pair. Repeat the stitch pattern four times. At the end of the round, step up through the first D added (figure 6).

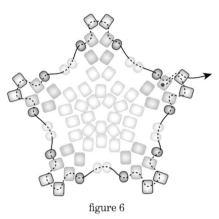

figure 6

Round 8: Add two Ds in herringbone stitch on top of the pair of Ds. Then peyote stitch one F and pass it through the next bead in the prior round. Repeat adding one F twice more. Then repeat the stitch pattern four times. At the end of the round, step up through the first D added (figure 7).

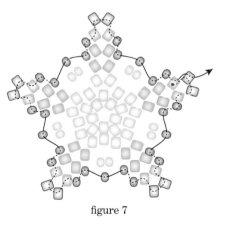

figure 7

Round 9: Add two Fs in herringbone stitch on top of the pair of Ds. Peyote stitch one F in the next stitch. Then, using three Hs, peyote stitch once, skipping over the middle F from the last round and stitching through the third. Finally, peyote stitch one F. Repeat the stitch pattern four times. At the end of the round, step up through the first F added (figure 8).

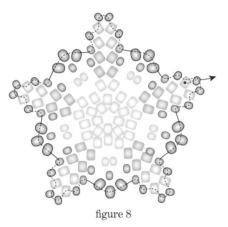

figure 8

Round 10: Add one F between the two Ds. Pick up one F and two Hs and peyote stitch once, passing through the middle H from the previous row. Pick up two Hs and one D and peyote stitch through the first F. Repeat the stitch pattern four times; then secure your thread in the beadwork and trim it. Secure your tail thread and trim it as well (figure 9).

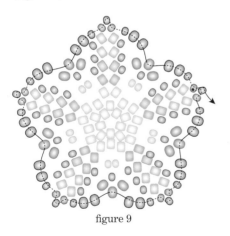

figure 9

Large Leaf

2 Start a new thread. Follow along with figure 10.

Column of beads. String 15 Js and three Gs and stitch back through the last three Js, forming a picot with the 15°s.

First set of veins. Pick up two Js and one G and stitch through all the beads in the picot. Pick up one G and two Js and stitch through the third, fourth, and fifth Js in the column of beads, counting from the bottom of the picot.

Second set of veins. Pick up four Js and one G and stitch through the last J from the previous group of beads on the right side; then go back through the beads just added and stitch up through the fifth J in the middle column of beads, where you started. Pick up four Js and one G and stitch through the last J in the previous group of beads; then go back through the beads just added. Stitch down three Js in the middle column.

Third set of veins. Pick up five Js and one G and stitch through the last J in the previous row on the right-hand side; then go back through the beads just added. Stitch up one J in the middle column. Add a row on the left-hand side identical to that on the right. Stitch down three Js in the middle column.

Fourth set of veins. Add the next row in the same way, using six Js and one G on each side.

Fifth set of veins. Add the next row the same way, using seven Js and one G on each side. Then stitch down only two beads in the middle column, instead of three.

Sixth set of veins. Pick up seven Js and one G. Stitch through the last J in the previous row on the right side; then stitch back through the beads just added. Stitch up one J in the middle row and add an identical row on the left-hand side. Stitch down three Js in the middle column.

Seventh set of veins. Pick up five Js and one G. Stitch through the second-to-last J in the previous row on the right-hand side; then go back through the beads just added. Stitch up one J in the middle column. Add an identical row; then stitch down two Js, bringing your thread out of the bottom of the leaf.

Bottom of leaf. Add one additional J on the bottom of the leaf; then secure the working thread in the beadwork and trim it. Reinforce the new J with your tail thread; then secure it in the beadwork and trim it.

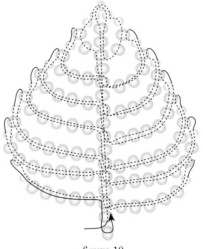

figure 10

Small Leaf

3 The small leaf is stitched much like the large leaf using Js and Gs, but includes fewer rows and fewer beads in each row. Follow figure 11 for the exact number.

figure 11

Large Tendril

4 Cut 3 inches (7.6 cm) of wire. Use your round-nose and chain-nose pliers to make a small simple loop at one end. Grasping the wire with your hand, work the wire around the end loop in an increasingly larger radius to form a spiral, leaving ½ inch (1.3 cm) of straight wire at the end (figure 12).

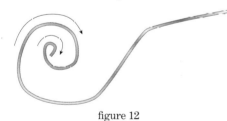

figure 12

5 String on Js to about ¼ inch (6 mm) from the end where the small loop is. Bend the wire at ¼ inch (6 mm) from the end; then make a simple loop slightly larger than the first loop with the remaining wire, so it has about a ⅛-inch (3 mm) inside diameter. Make sure the simple loop is closed completely (figure 13).

figure 13

Small Tendril

6 Make a small tendril like the large one but use wire that's 2¼ inches (5.7 cm) long.

Assemble the Earrings

7 Refer to figure 14 for the following steps.

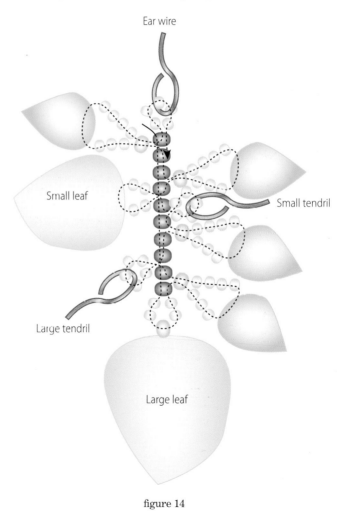

figure 14

Stem. Using one-half wingspan of thread, pick up 10 Ks, which form the main stem off of which you'll use fringing to add the components of the earring.

Large leaf. Pick up two Gs and stitch through the sideways J on the bottom of the large leaf. Pick up two Gs and stitch through the last K.

First glass leaf. Pick up one J, three Gs, and one glass leaf. Pick up four Gs and stitch back through the J and up through one K on the main stem.

Large tendril. Pick up five Gs and the large loop on the large tendril and stitch up through the next two Ks on the main stem.

Second glass leaf. Pick up one J, three Gs, and one glass leaf. Pick up four Gs and stitch back through the J and up through one K on the main stem.

Small tendril. Pick up five Gs and the large loop on the small tendril. Stitch up through the next K on the main stem.

Small leaf. Pick up two Gs and stitch through the sideways J on the bottom of the small leaf. Pick up two Gs and stitch up through the next K on the main stem.

Third glass leaf. Pick up one J, three Gs, and one glass leaf. Pick up four Gs and stitch back through the J and the next two Ks on the main stem.

Fourth glass leaf. Pick up one J, three Gs, and one glass leaf. Pick up four Gs and stitch back through the J and the next K on the main stem. Your thread should now be emerging from the end of the main stem.

Loop. Pick up five Gs and the bottom loop of one ear wire. Stitch down five Ks on the main stem.

8 Put the needle through the center of the morning glory (not through any beads), moving from back to front (figure 15). Pick up one 2-mm pearl and put the needle back through the morning glory. Stitch back through the second-to-last and last Ks on the main stem through which you had previously stitched. Take out any slack and tighten up your thread so that the flower sits horizontally along the main stem.

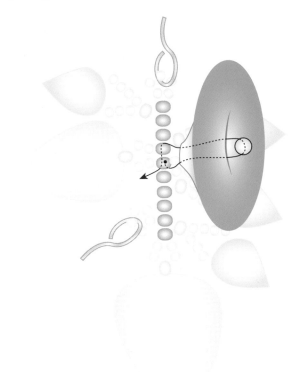

figure 15

Repeat the thread path at least once more to reinforce the stitching; then weave down to the large leaf to secure your thread before trimming it.

9 Repeat all steps to make a second earring.

A

B

A Melissa Grakowsky Shippee
Little Windows, 2012
20 x 10 cm
Seed beads, bicones, crystal stones,
crystal pearls; off-loom beadweaving
Photo by artist

B Melissa Grakowsky Shippee
Vernal Equinox Headdress, 2010
21 x 20 x 4 cm
Seed beads, bicones, crystal pearls, wire;
bead embroidery, wirework
Photo by artist

C

D

C Melissa Grakowsky Shippee
Tea Service, 2013
25 x 15 x 8 cm
Seed beads, bicones, ceramic teacups and
sugar bowl lid; off-loom beadweaving
Photo by artist

D Melissa Grakowsky Shippee
Progression, 2013
20 x 10 cm
Seed beads, crystal beads, wire, motor parts;
bead embroidery
Photo by artist

Anneta Valious

Photo by Alexis Brosseau

A self-taught jewelry maker, Anneta Valious was born and raised in Moscow. She studied psychology at the University of Moscow, but has now lived in France for many years with her husband and two children. Anneta inherited a love for crafting, along with a profound appreciation of beauty, from her mother and grandmother.

In 2007, while searching for a gift for their daughter, Anneta and her husband chose a box of seed beads. And that's how Anneta discovered the world of beading! She learned to beadweave and do bead embroidery from books and the Internet. It wasn't long before she became deeply passionate about creating her own soutache jewelry designs, and she now can't imagine life without beads. Anneta has written two books on soutache embroidery, one in Russian, and one in English called quite simply *Soutache*. See more of her work at www.annetavalious.com

Flitter Earrings

A pond in a meadow on a hazy summer day. Cattails sway languidly and a frog calls its deep, wet croak. A dragonfly darts here and there, its wings a dry rustle. It lands on a partly submerged branch.

SUPPLIES

Antique silver size 8° seed beads, 1 g

Mauve size 11° seed beads, 1 g

Size 11° cylinder beads:

    Antique silver, 1 g

    Violet, 1 g

    Matte blue AB, 1 g

Size 15° seed beads:

    Antique silver, 1 g

    Violet, 1 g

    Mauve, 1 g

50 violet opal crystal bicones, 3 mm

4 light pink crystal rondelles, 4 mm

2 violet crystal teardrops, 9 x 6 mm

2 palest blue heart-shaped faceted crystals, 12 mm

2 palest violet square crystal rhinestones, 10 mm or 12 mm, each set in a four-hole silver-colored bezel

Crystal pearls:

    8 lavender, 4 mm

    2 lavender, 6 mm

2 palest violet crystal chaton montées, 4 or 5 mm

5 inches (12.7 cm) of fine silver chain

Silver jump rings:

    8, 4 mm

    2 triangle-shaped, 5 mm

2 silver ear wires

2 pieces of synthetic suede, 1 x 2 inches (2.5 x 5.1 cm)

Gray nylon beading thread

2 yards (1.8 m) each of soutache in blue-gray and navy blue

2 Czech glass buttons with a dragonfly motif, 11/16 inch (1.7 cm)

7 inches (17.8 cm) of blue opal crystal rhinestone chain, 2.5 mm

2 pieces of navy blue leather, 1 x 2 inches (2.5 x 5.1 cm)

1 piece of tracing paper

Hypo jeweler's cement with needle-tip applicator

Size 12 needles, beading or sharps

Small, sharp scissors

Paper scissors

Black marking pen

Light-colored marking pen

Chain-nose pliers

Wire cutter

DIMENSIONS

1¹/₂ x 4¹/₂ inches (3.8 x 11.4 cm)

TECHNIQUES

Soutache embroidery (page 125)

Brick stitch (page 122)

Circular peyote stitch

INSTRUCTIONS

The instructions are for one earring. To help them match more closely, create both of them in tandem rather than completing one and then making the other.

Make the Button Component

1 If the button has a wire shank, use chain-nose pliers to fold it to the side to allow the button to rest flat on a surface, but leave enough space so that you can stitch through the shank. Thread the needle with an arm's length of thread, knot the end, and pass through one piece of synthetic suede, moving from back to front. Then stitch the button to the synthetic suede through the shank, ending with the thread at the component's back. Apply glue to the suede below the button and apply pressure to secure it. Allow to dry. **Note:** Avoid adding glue beyond the button's edge, because you'll be sewing down the rhinestone chain around the button and the glue can make it hard to get through the suede.

2 Using the leftover thread, stitch the rhinestone chain to the suede all around the button and use a wire cutter to snip off any extra. Trim the suede close to the edge of the rhinestone chain, making sure not to cut the thread. Secure the thread on the wrong side.

3 Cut a piece of blue-gray soutache 8 inches (20.3 cm) long. Stitch it completely around the rhinestone chain as shown in figures 1 through 3, making sure your needle passes exactly through the groove in the soutache. At the spot where the ends join, make a few stitches to reinforce the connection. **Note:** To avoid damaging the soutache, be careful not to force the thread through it.

4 Cut a piece of navy blue soutache 8 inches (20.3 cm) long. Attach it around the blue-gray soutache, making sure to keep your stitches invisible. (To achieve this, insert the needle at almost the same spot where you brought the thread out.)

5 Attach a rondelle on one side of the join. Wrap and stitch both layers of soutache around it, keeping your stitches invisible (figures 4 and 5). Right next to the rondelle, make a loop and sew a 4-mm pearl in it (figure 6). Repeat this step on the other side of the joined soutache.

6 Arrange the ends of the soutache side by side on the back of the beadwork, apply glue to them, and cut off any extra soutache (figures 7 and 8).

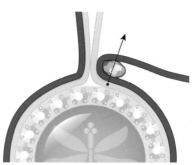

figure 4

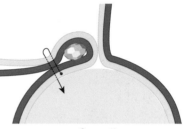

figure 5

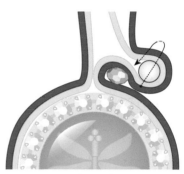

figure 6

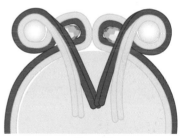

figure 7

figure 8

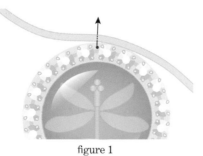

figure 1

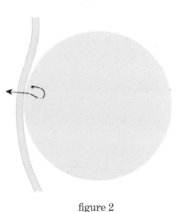

figure 2

figure 3

Make the Tear-drop Component

7 Cut a piece of navy blue soutache 4¾ inches (12 cm) long. Attach thread to it by making a knot in the end and passing the needle through the middle of the soutache, going back and forth with the needle several times. String on an 11° and a teardrop. Wrap the soutache around the beads; then bring the needle and thread through the soutache at the narrow end of the teardrop. Pass the needle back through the teardrop, the 11°, and the soutache (figure 9).

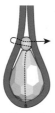

figure 9

Cut two more pieces of soutache, one blue-gray and one navy blue, both 4¾ inches (12 cm) long. Stitch them as shown in figure 10.

figure 10

8 Form loops on each side of the teardrop, and sew a 4-mm pearl inside each one. Tuck the ends of the soutache to the back of the component, apply glue to the soutache, press it to the component's back, and trim off any extra (figure 11).

figure 11

Assemble the Components

9 Before you join the button and the teardrop components, you need to make a paper pattern of the teardrop component. (The button component has a backing of beadwork [made in step 15], not leather.) Place it on a piece of tracing paper, right side up, and trace its shape on the paper using a black pen. Cut out the pattern. Then place it on the front of the leather and trace it onto the leather using a light-colored pen. Cut the shape out and set the resulting leather backing aside.

10 Use two 8°s to attach the button component to the teardrop component as shown in figure 12. In the empty space at the center, string on and attach an antique silver 15°, a 6-mm pearl, and another antique silver 15° (figure 13).

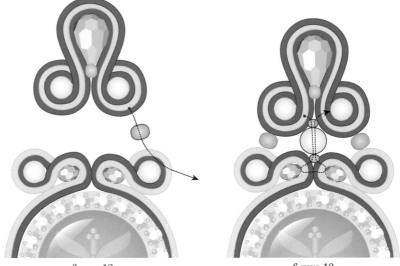

figure 12   figure 13

11 Cut a new piece of thread, knot it, and pass it from the back to the front of the work. Embellish around the bottom of the button as follows.

Row 1. Using brick stitch, stitch on a row of 8°s, as shown in figure 14. **Note:** In this case, you pass your needle through the edge of the component instead of passing under the thread from a prior row.

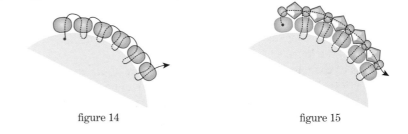

figure 14   figure 15

Row 2. Turn your work around and string one antique silver 15°, one bicone, and one antique silver 15°. Then pass the thread through the second 8° from the one that you just exited, through the suede, and back up through the same 8° to create a picot (figure 15). Pass the thread back through the last 15° to cause it to stand upright. *String on a bicone and a 15°, then go through the next 8° and the suede. Go back up through the same 8° and the 15° just above it. Repeat from * across the bottom of the component. Pass the thread through the back of the work, make several small stitches to secure it, and cut it.

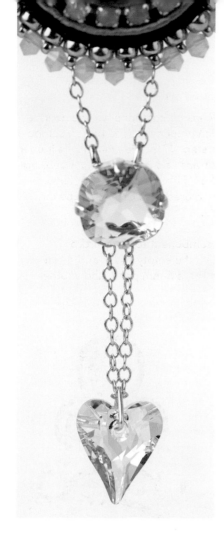

Attach the loose end of the long piece of chain to the bottom of the bezel, just beside the other end.

Add the Backing

13 To attach the leather backing to each teardrop component, make a knot in the thread and secure it to the back of the beadwork. Pass the needle under the outermost row of soutache and exit from the groove on the edge of the piece. Place the backing in position. Insert the needle in the same spot that it exits the soutache and catch the backing ⅛ inch (3 mm) from the edge. Stitch back through the trim, coming out through the groove. Pull the thread. The edge of the backing will bury itself under the final row of soutache as you stitch. Make every stitch ¹⁄₁₆ to ⅛ inch (1.6 to 3 mm) from the edge of the lining and from the preceding stitch (figures 16 and 17). Stitch all around to attach the backing to the beadwork.

When you finish, poke the needle between the backing and the soutache. Pull the needle through the backing but don't go all the way. Apply a smidge of glue to the thread, close to the backing. Now pull the thread through it. The glue will help secure the thread where it's hidden under the backing. Repeat this process several times before cutting the thread (figure 18).

14 Pass an ear wire through the soutache at the top of the teardrop component, going through the loop in the component.

15 Following along with figure 19, use circular peyote stitch to create a back for the button component, as follows. **Note:** As you work, check the size of this piece against the back of the button component and make adjustments as necessary.

12 Add a crystal pendant to the bottom of the assembled components as follows, using the photo above as reference. First cut a piece of chain 1½ inches (3.8 cm) long and two pieces ⅜ inch (1 cm) long.

Top crystal (square rhinestone). Using 4-mm jump rings, attach one end of each of the shorter pieces of chain through the holes in the bezel that holds the rhinestone, with one on each side. We'll consider this side the top. Stitch the loose ends of the short pieces of chain to the soutache behind the violet bicones. Attach just one end of the longer piece of chain on the bottom of the bezel.

Bottom crystal (heart). Using a triangle-shaped jump ring as a bail, pass it around the hole in a heart-shaped crystal; then pass the long chain through the triangle-shaped jump ring. **Note:** Don't run the triangle-shaped jump ring through a link. The crystal should be able to move freely along the chain.

figure 16

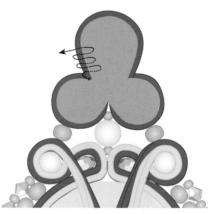

figure 17

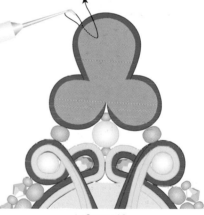

figure 18

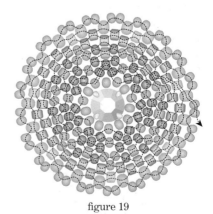

figure 19

Round 4. Peyote stitch the round, using one violet 15° for each stitch.

Round 5. Peyote stitch the round, using a pattern of one stitch with one violet cylinder bead and one stitch with two antique silver 15°s. *Note:* Place the cylinder beads between the violet 15°s in the prior round and place the two antique silver 15°s above the antique silver 15°s from Round 3. Again, you're performing the first step of an increase in this round when you add two beads in a stitch. You should have 21 beads in the round.

Round 6. Peyote stitch the round, using a pattern of two stitches with one violet 15° and one stitch with one antique silver 15°. The order, again, is important. Place the antique silver 15° between the two antique silver 15°s from the previous round. You're completing the increases from the prior round in this round.

Round 7. Peyote stitch the round, using one matte blue cylinder bead for each stitch.

Round 8. Peyote stitch the round, using a pattern of one stitch with one antique silver cylinder bead and two stitches with one matte blue cylinder bead. The order is, again, important. Place the silver cylinder beads above the antique silver 15°s from round 5.

Round 9. Peyote stitch the round, using one 11° in each stitch.

Round 10. Peyote stitch the round, using two antique silver 15°s in each stitch. This round should have 42 beads.

16 Cut a new piece of thread, make a knot in it, and stitch the element made in step 15 to the back of the button component, going through the beads on the edge of the element as needed and passing through them several times to make the connections secure.

Round 1. Holding the chaton montée, pick up an antique silver 15° and pass the thread through a hole in it and back through the 15°. Repeat around the chaton montée until you've surrounded it with 14 beads. You want the 15°s to lie parallel to the edge of the chaton montée because you'll be using these beads as the base round for circular peyote stitch.

Round 2. Using two violet 15°s for each stitch, peyote stitch the round. You're performing the first step of an increase in this round when you add two beads in a stitch. You need to include these increases so the circular peyote stitch will continue to be flat.

Round 3. Alternating one antique silver 15° and one violet 15°, peyote stitch the round. *Note:* The order in which you use the different colors is important. The violet 15°s should lie between the two violet 15°s from the previous round. When adding one bead between two beads from the prior step in this round, you're completing the increases. Therefore, the violet 15°s in this round are the beads that complete the increases.

SUPPLIES

Matte olive size 11° Delicas, 5 g

Size 11° seed beads:

    Iridescent green, 1 g

    Gold, 2 g

Size 15° seed beads:

    Gold, 1 g

    Transparent olive green, 5 g

50 iridescent green bicones, 3 mm

2 clear rivolis, 14 mm

2 light topaz crystal teardrops,
    9 x 6 mm

12 pyrite round beads, 6 mm

26 to 28 gold-colored metal
    rondelles, 5 mm

4 palest gold faceted crystal
    rondelles, 4 mm

1 green opal oval cabochon,
    3.5 x 2 cm

1 gold three-hole clasp

1 piece of gray synthetic suede,
    1 x 2 inches (2.5 x 5.1 cm)

Gray nylon beading thread

2¼ yards (2 m) of light gray
    soutache

1 piece of light brown leather,
    2 x 4 inches (5.1 x 10.2 cm)

Hypo jeweler's cement with
    needle-tip applicator

Synthetic stuffing (optional)

1 sheet of tracing paper

Size 12 needles, beading or sharps

Sharp embroidery scissors

Paper scissors

Black marking pen

Light-colored marking pen

DIMENSIONS

7 x 2 inches (17.8 x 5.1 cm)

TECHNIQUES

Backstitch (page 124)

Tubular even-count peyote stitch
    (page 120)

Soutache embroidery (page 125)

Embellishing

Flat odd-count peyote stitch
    (page 121)

Fairy Queen Bracelet

Draping your wrist in graceful tendrils of soutache embroidery and narrow arcs of peyote stitching, this romantic piece has a delicate, ethereal quality. Light glinting off the crystals could almost be mistaken for dewdrops. Is that a wee winged imp hiding among the beads?

INSTRUCTIONS

Create a Bezel for the Cabochon

1 Glue the cabochon to the suede.

2 Knot your thread and bring the needle up from the back of the suede, close to the edge of the cabochon. Working in 2-1 backstitch, completely surround the cabochon with a round of Delicas, making sure to keep the quantity an even number.

3 Peyote stitch the round using one Delica per stitch. This stitching will form a ring containing three rounds of beads. If your cab is rather tall, add more rounds of Delicas as needed. **Note:** In peyote stitch, the beads that you string become the first and second round. In this case, the Delicas in the backstitched round act as the initial string and become rounds 1 and 2 of the tube. At the end of a round in even-count tubular peyote stitch, you need to pass through the first bead of the current round, or step up, to begin the next round.

Still working in peyote stitch, step up and add a round of gold 15°s. This round will cause the bezel to tighten against the cab, holding it in position. Pass the thread through the last round again to strengthen and tighten the beading. Weave your thread through the beads in the bezel and bring it out on the back of the suede.

Embellish around the Cabochon

4 Bring the thread back up to the suede's front just next to the bezel's base and, using 1-1 backstitch, add one round of green 11°s around the exterior of the bezel (figure 1). Pass the thread to the back of the suede.

5 Pass the thread back up to the front at the middle of the cabochon on one side. Stitch a pyrite bead right next to the cabochon on both sides. Then stitch a round of rondelles around the open edge of each pyrite bead. Pass the thread to the back of the suede.

6 Bringing the thread to the top of the suede just above the rondelles around one pyrite bead, use 1-1 backstitch to add bicones around the top of the cabochon, stopping at the rondelles just above the pyrite bead on the other side. Pass your thread to the back of the suede and then to the front again, just below the same pyrite bead. Repeat adding bicones around the bottom of the cabochon (figure 2). Cut off the extra suede right along the edge of the bead embroidery, but be careful not to cut any threads.

7 Cut a piece of soutache 4¾ inches (12 cm) long. Sew it along the edge of bicones at the top of the cabochon, starting above the pyrite bead on one side and moving to the same position on the opposite side (figure 3). Make sure to pass your needle through the suede and through the groove in the soutache, and to use tiny stitches that aren't visible.

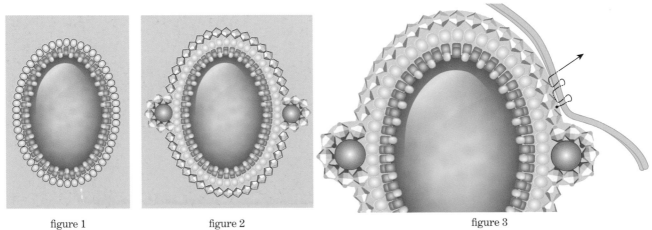

figure 1   figure 2   figure 3

Cut another piece of soutache 4¾ inches (12 cm) long and attach this second row above the first row.

8 As shown in figure 4, sew crystal rondelles on both sides near the pyrite beads. Wrap both layers of soutache around them. Tuck the ends of the soutache on both sides to the back of the work. Cut off the soutache, leaving ends ½ inch (1.3 cm) long.

figure 4

9 Repeat adding two rows of soutache and rondelles to the bottom of the cabochon (figure 5).

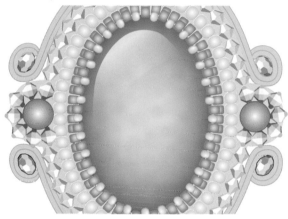

figure 5

10 Cut four pieces of soutache 1¾ inches (4.4 cm) long. Sew two pieces around each of the pyrite beads that are surrounded by rondelles (figures 6 and 7).

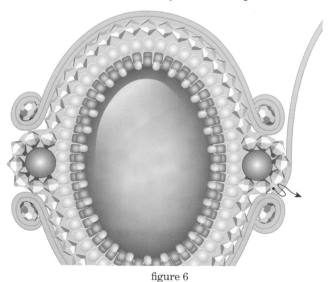

figure 6

figure 7

Make the Rivoli Components

11 Create a bezel for one rivoli in even-count peyote stitch, using 36 Delicas (page 121).

12 Cut a piece of soutache 12 inches (30.5 cm) long. Position the rivoli in the middle of the piece of soutache. As shown in figure 8, stitch the soutache around the second round of Delicas in the bezel that surrounds the rivoli. Then stitch in a green 11° next to the bezel where the ends of the soutache join (figure 9).

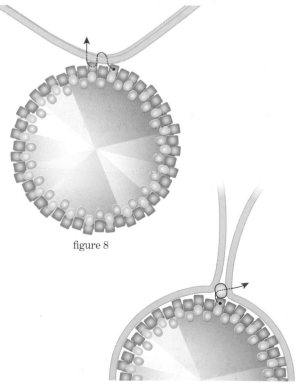

figure 8

figure 9

Attach a second row of soutache to the first, making sure to keep your stitching invisible. Fold back the outer row of soutache and use it to attach a row of gold 11°s halfway around the rivoli to the point opposite where you added the green 11° in step 11 (figure 10). Repeat adding gold 11°s, using the same row of soutache on the other side of the rivoli. Where the ends of the soutache meet, attach a 3-mm bicone between the gold 11°s on either side (figure 11).

14 Cut a piece of soutache 2 inches (5.1 cm) long. Thread your needle with an arm's length of thread and make a knot in the end of the thread. String on one gold 11° and a crystal teardrop. Surround these beads with the piece of soutache and pass your needle through the soutache at the narrow end of the teardrop. Go back through the teardrop, the 11°, and the soutache. Cut another piece of soutache of the same size and attach it around the first, making sure to keep your stitching invisible (figure 15).

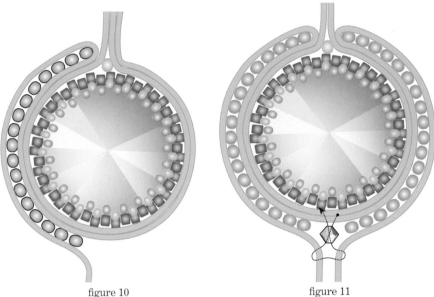

figure 10   figure 11

Stitch the innermost layer of soutache to the outermost. Make a few careful stitches where the four ends of soutache join up to reinforce that spot (figure 12).

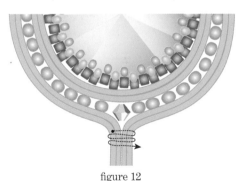

figure 12

figure 15

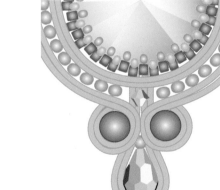

figure 16

13 On one side of the join, sew on a pyrite bead. Wrap two ends of the soutache around it. Repeat adding a pyrite bead on the other side. Make a few stitches to attach the soutache behind the rivoli, coat the ends of the soutache with glue, and cut off any excess (figures 13 and 14).

15 As shown in figure 16, attach the element made in step 14 behind the one completed in steps 11, 12, and 13.

16 Repeat steps 11 to 14 to make a second rivoli component.

Assemble the Components

17 Before you join the components, you need to take a paper pattern from them. Place each component on a piece of tracing paper, right side up, and draw its shape on the paper using a black marking pen. Cut out the patterns. Then place them on the front of the leather and trace their pattern using a light-colored marking pen. Cut the shape out of the leather. Set aside this leather backing.

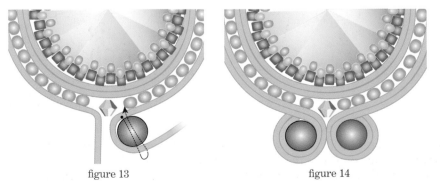

figure 13   figure 14

18 Attach the rivoli components to the cabochon component using pyrite beads. Also using pyrite beads, attach each half of the clasp to the rivoli components.

19 Use flat uneven-count peyote stitch to make a decorative arc of beadweaving, as follows. With your thread coming out of the soutache surrounding the cabochon, string on 23 to 25 Delicas. (This quantity will vary depending on the size and shape of the cabochon.) Then go through the soutache surrounding one of the rivoli components (figure 17).

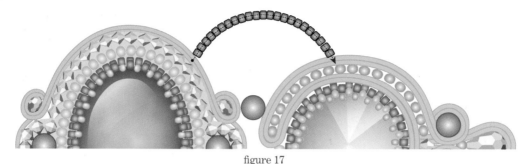

figure 17

Peyote stitch two rows of green 15°s on the interior of the arc and one row of gold 11°s on the exterior.

20 Make seven other decorative arcs between the cabochon component and the rivoli components and between the rivoli components and the clasp (figure 18). Peyote stitch between components with 11°s and 15°s for the exterior arcs and string rondelles and bicones between components for the interior arcs.

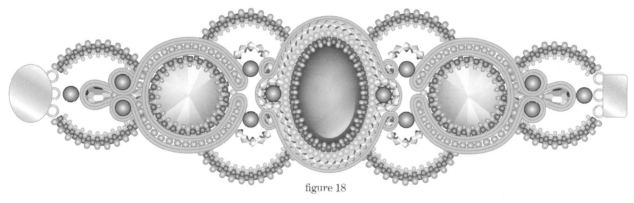

figure 18

Add the Backing

If empty pockets between the beads and the leather backing cause dimples in the leather, fill them with a bit of stuffing before you stitch down the leather.

21 Make a knot in the thread and secure it to the back of the beadwork. Pass the needle under the outermost row of soutache and exit from the groove on the edge of the piece. Place the leather backing in position. Insert the needle in the same spot that it exits the soutache and catch the backing ⅛ inch (3 mm) from the edge. Stitch back through the trim, coming out through the groove. Pull the thread. The edge of the backing will bury itself under the final row of soutache as you stitch. Make every stitch ⅟₁₆ to ⅛ inch (1.6 to 3 mm) from the edge of the lining and from the preceding stitch (figures 19 and 20).

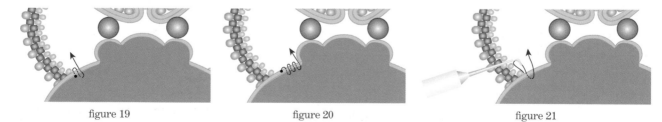

figure 19   figure 20   figure 21

Stitch all around to attach the backing to the beadwork. Poke the needle between the backing and the soutache and pull it only partly through the backing. Apply a smidge of glue to the thread, close to the backing, then pull the thread through. Repeat several times, then cut the thread (figure 21). Don't forget to add backings to the rivoli components.

A

B

C

A **Anneta Valious**
Skyfall, 2013
40 x 18 cm
Calcite, Swarovski stones
and pearls, soutache, leather;
soutache embroidery
Photo by artist

B **Anneta Valious**
Jurassic, 2013
45 x 24 cm
Agate, glass beads, seed beads,
drops, soutache, leather;
soutache embroidery,
peyote stitch
Photo by artist

C **Anneta Valious**
Inconnue (Unknown), 2013
20 x 18 cm
Pearls, Swarovski beads,
seed beads, rhinestone
chain, soutache, lace, leather;
soutache embroidery,
peyote stitch
Photo by artist

Techniques

This book assumes that you have some experience with beading, so the information in this section serves mostly as a refresher.

GLOSSARY OF TERMS

Arm's Length. A length of thread as long as the distance between your chin and the tips of your fingers when you have one arm outstretched, usually equivalent to 1 yard (91.4 cm).

Bail. A finding that attaches a pendant to a necklace or other jewelry.

Basting. Sewing with loose temporary stitches.

Down Bead. Generally used in peyote stitch, refers to a bead that's lower than the bead in the current row. In the case of peyote stitch, the down beads are the ones in the second-to-last row stitched.

Foundation. The material on which you do bead embroidery. You then cover its back with a material such as Ultrasuede to cover your stitches.

Picot. An ornamental edging where a number of beads form a triangular shape.

Stepping Up. The act of stitching through the first bead in a round or a row, depending on the stitch you're using, which gets you into position to start the next round or row.

Stopper Bead versus Stop Bead. These terms are often used interchangeably and can refer to two different things. In this book, a stopper is the one bead at the end of a strand of beads—such as a fringe—that keeps all of the other beads from coming off the end. A stop bead, on the other hand, is a bead strung before the rest of the beads to prevent the first few beads from falling off, as well as to establish thread tension. After adding a stop bead as directed, slide it along the thread so it's roughly 6 inches (15.2 cm) from the end and tie the thread around it. This thread should hold the bead in place so that you can accomplish enough of the stitching to establish the beadwork. Then remove the stop bead.

Stitching in the Ditch. Adding beads on top of a completed row of stitching, generally to embellish the beadwork or to make it stronger. See page 121.

Tacking. Making several small stitches on the foundation, until the thread is secure enough that it doesn't pull out.

Up Bead. Generally used in peyote stitch, refers to a bead that sticks out further than the ones around it. In the case of peyote, the up beads are the ones in the last row stitched.

Wingspan. A length of thread as long as the distance between the tips of your fingers when you have your arms outstretched.

Zipping. Joining two edges that have beads that are offset and that mesh together like the teeth in a zipper.

Basic Skills

CONDITIONING THREAD

Before you start working with a new thread, you might want pull it through beeswax, microcrystalline wax, or commercial thread conditioner. Doing so can help reduce tangling, depending on the thread and the product. Beeswax and microcrystalline wax also can help make beadwork stiffer, if necessary. As you keep going through beads, some of the coating will wear off, so you'll need to condition from time to time.

MAINTAINING TENSION

When you start a project, wind the tail of the thread four or five times around your nondominant pinkie. This allows you to tug on the thread when you string beads, to keep the beadwork tight. Pull not just on the working thread but on the tail for the first half-dozen rows or rounds. You can unwind the thread when you've done enough stitching that the beads won't fall off at the tail.

As you work, and especially when directed to do so in instructions, reinforce loose stitching by following your initial thread path a second time. If you naturally stitch at a loose tension and want to stiffen the beadwork, you can wax the thread or use it doubled. If you find that your beadwork is too stiff, don't pull so hard on the stitching as you bead and don't use wax.

ADDING NEW THREADS

When you add thread, you need to secure it. Beaders use various techniques to start a new thread for beadweaving, such as peyote stitch, and for bead embroidery on a foundation. For whatever technique you use, stop when you have only 6 inches (15.2 cm) of thread left.

For beadweaving. Cut a new piece of thread and thread it onto a needle. Then pass it through a bead near the bead where the old thread is exiting and weave it through the nearby beads, changing direction several times to make it secure. Then exit from the bead out of which the old thread is exiting, with the new thread going in the same direction as the old thread. Continue weaving using the new thread. (The next section tells you how to end the old thread.)

For bead embroidery. Some beaders just knot the end and pass the needle through the foundation, moving from back to front. Others make small stitches through the back of the foundation until the thread doesn't come out when pulled on hard. Then they pass the needle to the front of the work.

FINISHING THREADS

When you finish thread, you also need to secure it. For beadweaving such as peyote stitch, weaving in tails when you start a project or add a thread can help combat fraying. To do so, remove any stop beads. Thread the tail onto a needle and weave it through the nearby beads, changing direction several times to make it secure. When you finish a thread, use the same method. To make the thread more secure, you can also pass it through some beads, tie a half-hitch knot (shown at right), pass through a few more beads, and trim off the remaining thread with scissors or a thread burner.

For bead embroidery on a foundation, some beaders just knot the end and cut the thread. Others make small stitches through the back of the foundation and cut the thread.

KNOTS

Overhand Knot

Half-Hitch Knot

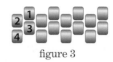

Square Knot

Beadweaving Stitches

PEYOTE STITCH

This is probably the most popular stitch among beaders.

Flat Even-Count Peyote Stitch

1 String on an even amount of beads; the example shows eight. This string of beads becomes the first and second row of the peyote stitch. For the third row, pick up a bead, skip the next one, and pass through the next bead. Continue this pattern for the rest of the row (figure 1). Note how some beads are up beads, and some are down beads.

figure 1

2 Now you'll start the fourth row. Pick up a bead, reverse direction and pass through the first up bead. Pick up a bead, skip the next one, and pass through the next up bead. Continue this pattern for the rest of the row (figure 2).

figure 2

If you lose track of how many rows you've made, count them on the diagonal in a zig-zag pattern, as shown in figure 3.

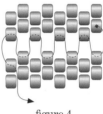

figure 3

Zipping
Make a flat piece of even-count peyote, fold the piece into a tube, and weave through the up beads on each side to zip the tube closed (figure 4).

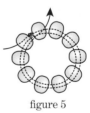

figure 4

Tubular Even-Count Peyote Stitch
Each round will stack on the second-to-last round to form a tube.

Rounds 1 and 2. String the required amount of beads—10 in this example—and pass through them all again to form a ring. The beads in this ring become the first and second rounds. Make a double knot; then pass the thread through the very first bead strung (figure 5).

figure 5

Round 3. Pick up one bead, skip a bead in the ring, and pass through the next bead (figure 6). Repeat this pattern all the way around to add a total of five beads in this round (figure 7).

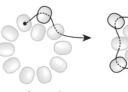

figure 6   figure 7

Pass through the first bead of the previous round to complete this round. Then pass through the first bead of the round to step up.

Round 4. Pick up one bead, skip a bead, and pass through the next up bead, that is, a bead added in the prior round. Repeat this pattern all the way around to add a total of five beads in this round.

Pass through the first bead of the just-finished round to step up. Repeat Round 4 until the tube is the desired length.

Stepping Up in Peyote Stitch
In both flat and tubular even-count peyote stitch, you need to step up at the end of a row or round to get to the next stitch. To step up in tubular even-count peyote, add the last bead as usual, passing through the last bead of the previous round; then pass through the first bead added in the current round. To step up in flat even-count peyote, on the other hand, add the last bead as usual, passing through the first bead of the previous row. String a bead, then pass through the last bead added in the previous row.

Flat Odd-Count Peyote Stitch
This stitch is done in the same way as flat even-count peyote stitch, except for the turn on one side.

1 String on an odd number of beads; the example shows seven. Begin as you would for even-count peyote stitch. When you're ready to pick up the last bead of the row, you won't have a bead through which you can pass the thread. To complete the last stitch, follow figure 8, starting at the red dot. Pick up a bead, pass through the bead directly above it, and then follow the thread path—a sort of figure eight—that the illustration shows.

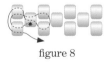
figure 8

2 Complete the next row as you would for even-count peyote (figure 9).

figure 9

Stitching in the Ditch
Use this technique for embellishing or building outward. With your thread exiting a bead, pick up a bead, outlined in red in figure 10, and pass through the next bead in the row.

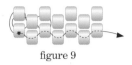
figure 10

Peyote Stitching a Bezel around a Rivoli

1 Thread your needle with an arm's length of thread. Pick up the amount of Delicas given in the instructions or exactly enough to go around the widest point of the rivoli. This amount should be an even number; if it's not, add—don't subtract—a bead to make it even. Pass through the first two beads strung to make a ring (figure 11).

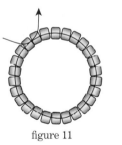
figure 11

2 Pick up a bead, skip a bead, and pass through the next bead. Repeat this pattern, working your way around the ring. You now have three rounds of beads, because the initial ring of peyote stitch always becomes rounds 1 and 2, and the Delicas added in this step become round 3. *Note:* Beginning at the end of round 3, and in every subsequent round, pass into the first bead of the current round to step up.

3 Switching to 15° seed beads, stitch two rounds of peyote stitch (figure 12). As you add each bead, pull on both threads. This tension will cause the beadwork to cup.

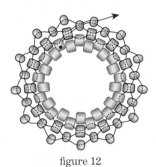
figure 12

4 Weave to the very first round of beads from the original ring. Place the rivoli face up into the half-finished bezel.

5 Using strong thread tension and holding the rivoli in place with your fingers, peyote stitch two more rounds of 15° seed beads against the top of the rivoli (figure 13). Secure the thread by passing again through all the beads in the last round of 15° beads. Don't cut the tails just yet. You might want to use them later to attach the bezeled stone to the rest of the beadwork.

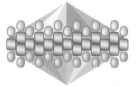
figure 13

RIGHT ANGLE WEAVE

This very popular stitch results in a supple fabric of beads. In its simplest form, RAW is a series of square units that share beads, thereby forming a grid. Each side can use one or more beads; therefore, each unit consists of at least four beads. The angles of the square are 90°, or right angles, hence the name of the stitch.

You'll weave the units alternately clockwise and counterclockwise; for rows, work back and forth.

Flat Right Angle Weave

1 To make the first unit, string four beads and pass through them all again clockwise to form a ring (figure 14). You should be exiting bead 4.

figure 14

2 To make the second unit, string three beads and, going counterclockwise, pass through beads 4, 5, and 6—the side of the first unit and the bottom and other side of the current unit (figure 15). **Note:** You'll always pass through the new side bead—in this case, bead 6—before beginning the next unit.

figure 15

3 Follow along with figure 16. For the third unit, pick up three beads. Going clockwise, pass through beads 6, 8, and 9—the side of the previous unit and the top and other side of this unit. Then to make the fourth unit, string three beads and go counterclockwise to pass through beads 9, 11, and 12, that is, the side of the previous unit and the bottom and other side of this unit. Notice how you've been alternating between clockwise and counterclockwise from unit to unit. Continue in this manner until you've made as many units as instructed.

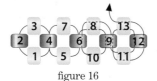

figure 16

Next, you need to get into position to begin a new row; you need to be exiting the top bead of the current row. Weave through bead 13. If you're in a unit where you're going clockwise, weave through the beads in the established direction until you get to the right place. The units in rows will share either the top or bottom bead or both if you've got a number of rows.

4 To make the first unit in the next row, pick up three beads, then pass clockwise through bead 13, which is the top bead of the previous row, and bead 14 (figure 17).

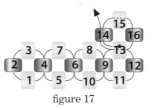

figure 17

5 To make the second unit in this row, pick up only two beads. Pass counterclockwise through bead 8, the top bead of the previous row; through bead 14, the side bead of the previous unit; and through beads 17 and 18. Then go through bead 7 to begin the next unit (figure 18).

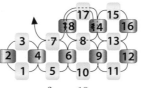

figure 18

6 You'll complete the row by continuing to pick up two beads for each unit, passing through previous beads and moving across in an alternating clockwise and counterclockwise direction. Don't forget that you need to end the last unit in position to begin the next row (figure 19).

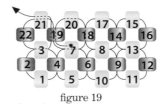

figure 19

7 To make the first unit in the next row, pick up three beads. You'll always pick up three beads for the first unit of subsequent rows. Then pass clockwise through bead 21, the top bead of the previous row; through the beads you just picked up—23, 24, and 25—and through bead 20, which is the top bead of the unit in the previous row (figure 20).

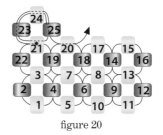

figure 20

Continue in this fashion until you've made the desired length.

LADDER STITCH

This version is also known as single-needle ladder stitch. Another type called double-needle ladder stitch looks identical but uses…you guessed it, two needles in a criss-crossing thread path.

1 String two beads and pass through them both again (figure 21).

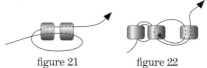

figure 21   figure 22

2 Position the beads so that they're side-by-side, with their holes parallel and vertical. With the thread exiting from the bottom of the second bead, pick up one bead, go down through the second bead, and then go up through the bead just added (figure 22). Repeat this thread path to keep adding beads as instructed.

BRICK STITCH

1 Make a bead ladder by following all the instructions for ladder stitch, using the amount of beads given in the instructions.

2 String on two beads, pass under the second connecting thread (shown in red in figure 23), and go up through the second bead just strung.

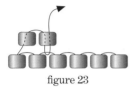

figure 23

String on a bead, pass under the next connecting thread, and go back up through the bead just strung (figure 24). Repeat this pattern until you reach the end of the row.

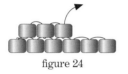

figure 24

To start the next row, flip the piece over so that you'll once again be working from left to right, and repeat step 2. *Reminder:* Always begin each row by stringing on two beads so the thread doesn't show on the edge.

SQUARE STITCH

1 Pick up a stopper bead, shown in orange. Then string on the desired amount of beads; the example uses five.

2 Pick up one bead, shown in green. Going counter-clockwise, pass through the corresponding bead in the row below, then pass through the bead just added (figure 25).

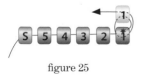

figure 25

Repeat until you've reached the end of the row (figure 26).

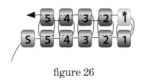

figure 26

To tighten the tension, pass through all the beads in the previous row from left to right, then pass through all the beads in the current row from right to left (figure 27).

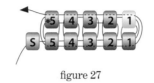

figure 27

3 Repeat step 2, but in the opposite direction across the row.

Bead Embroidery

Even if you follow the instructions and use the same materials as are listed for a project, you'll have to plan your own design for some projects. Also, the design may evolve as you bead, so it won't ever look exactly like the item in the photo. That's the nature of bead embroidery. A few broad guidelines for how to work follow.

1 Sketch your design on paper; then transfer it to the foundation and cut it out. If you're going to use transparent or pale beads, don't use a black pen; it might show through the beads in the finished piece. If you're using a foundation material that will fray, apply a no-fray treatment to the edges.

2 Glue on and/or sew the largest components or focal elements to the foundation first.

3 Continue adding beads from largest to smallest.

4 After stitching on all the beads, attach the outer backing.

5 Bead or otherwise finish the edge. This finish not only embellishes the piece, it joins the foundation and outer backing.

6 Complete the project by adding flourishes such as fringe, picots, or ruffles of beads; then attach any other components.

ADHESIVES

You can glue on any component that has a flat back, such as a cabochon. Use a craft adhesive to attach different materials, like stone and fabric, to each other. (Check the label to make sure it lists both of the materials you plan to stick together.) Before gluing, make sure the glue is clear when it dries and is flexible. A glue such as Aleene's Original Tacky Glue works well. Glue won't be enough to hold things on permanently. You'll also need to use bead-embroidery techniques to encase part of the component and secure it to the foundation material. To bond components permanently, use an industrial-strength adhesive like E-6000.

STITCHES

Whipstitch

1 Place the two layers of material together with their edges matching. Stitching near the edge, push your threaded needle straight up through the top layer and pull the thread.

2 Looping the thread around the edge and making this next stitch 1/8 inch (3 mm) from the previous one, push your needle up from the bottom through both layers. Pull the thread. Repeat around the beadwork (figure 28).

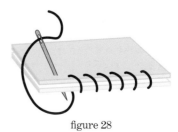

figure 28

One-Bead Stitch

1 Place the bead in position with its hole parallel to the foundation.

2 Stitch up from the back of the foundation to the top, just next to one side of the bead near the hole. Stitch through the bead and down to the back, just under the other side of the bead at the hole. Repeat (figure 29).

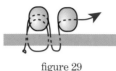

figure 29

For beads larger than size 11°, repeat the thread path again. Stitch up through the backing next to where the bead touches the surface and just beside your first stitch. Stitch through the bead and down to the back, just under the other side of the bead, at the hole as in the first pass. These side-by-side stitches will stabilize the bead. Proceed with this method for your next bead.

Backstitch
You can use this stitch to cover a surface in rows while creating patterns, either straight lines, scallops, or crosshatching. These directions describe two-bead backstitch that has a 2-3 pattern, but you can use other patterns, such as 1-1, 2-2, or 4-2 backstitch. The first number indicates how many beads to pick up when stitching forward; the second tells how many beads to count backward before stitching up to the top.

1 With your thread coming out of the right side of the foundation, string on two beads. Position them firmly against the foundation in the direction you want them to lie. Immediately next to the second bead, push your needle down perpendicularly through the foundation and pull the thread tight.

2 On the underside, push your needle up through the foundation next to the bead indicated by the stitch pattern that you're using, and go through the bead or beads again (figure 30).

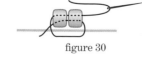

figure 30

For example, in 2-1 backstitch, you go through only the second bead added in the first stitch before stringing two beads for the next stitch. In 2-2 backstitch, you go through the two beads added in the first stitch. For 2-3 and greater, you go through two beads only in the first stitch and start the pattern at the second stitch.

3 String on two beads and push them snugly against the previous two beads, again positioning them firmly against the foundation in the direction you want them to go. Push your needle down through the foundation and pull the thread tight.

4 Push the beads back into the position where you want them to create a smooth-looking row. On the underside, come back up between the first and second beads and pass through the second, third, and fourth beads (figure 31).

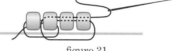

figure 31

5 Repeat as desired, stringing on two beads and coming back through three each time. Instead of stitching back and forth to create the rows, work in only one direction. To do so, after reaching the end of a row, go down to the back and then back up in the same spot. Without pulling the thread too tight, stitch back through the holes in the beads to get back to the starting point. This process also helps line up the beads into smooth-looking rows.

Stitch down to the underside; then go back up to the right side with your needle in the starting position for the next row.

Stacks Stitch
(aka Fringe Stitch or Stop Stitch)
This stitch is much like attaching fringe to the edge of beadwork, but you do it in the middle of the foundation. It produces a very different texture from backstitch, where the bead holes are parallel to the foundation.

1 With your thread on the front side of the foundation, pick up the desired amount of stack beads—possibly just one—plus a stopper, which is usually a seed bead. Push all the beads down the thread and snugly against the foundation.

2 Skipping the stopper, take your needle back through the stack bead(s) and through the foundation. Holding the stopper with one hand, carefully pull the thread with the other hand to adjust the tension.

3 Stitch back to the right side with your needle, in position to start the next stitch. Figure 32 shows a number of stacks made side by side.

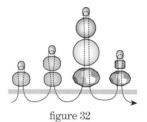

figure 32

You can use many stack beads in each stitch, but they'll be heavy, which can stress the foundation and cause it to tear later. To balance the weight, you need to provide an adequate base between stacks stitches. To do so, when you finish one stack, stitch over the width of several stacks to start the next one. Fill in empty areas with additional stacks stitches later, again stitching over the width of several stacks to start the next one, as shown in figure 33.

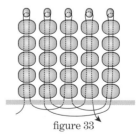

figure 33

Standard Edge Stitch
(aka Sunshine Edge, Brick Stitch Edge, or Single Bead Edge)
This creates a row of beads that camouflages the trimmed edge while attaching the backing and outer backing together.

1 Stitch through the edge to create a loop to secure the tail, or add a stop bead with a 9-inch (22.9 cm) tail thread. Pick up one bead. Stitch from the top to the back, at least ⅛ inch (3 mm) from the edge. Stitch up through the bead and pull (figure 34).

figure 34

2 Pick up one bead. Stitch through the backings and up through the bead (figure 35). Repeat this along the entire edge. When you're near your starting point, remove the loop stitch (or stop bead) and continue stitching until you reach the first bead in the row (figure 36).

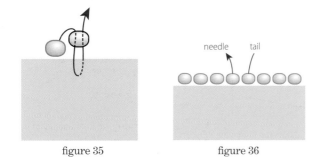

figure 35

figure 36

3 Pass the needle thread through the very first bead you stitched on; then add a needle to the tail thread and stitch through the last bead you stitched on (figure 37). Stitch both threads to the back (figure 38). Tie a square knot, weave in the threads, and cut.

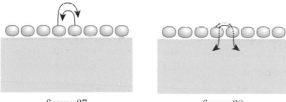

figure 37

figure 38

BEZELS

These differ from beadweaving bezels because they're built on a foundation material. Begin by gluing the cabochon or other such component to the foundation.

Even-Count Peyote stitch Bezel

1 After the adhesive has dried, backstitch an even number of beads around the component. With the needle coming straight up from the underside, pass through one of the backstitched beads.

2 Pick up a bead, skip the next bead in the base round of backstitched beads, and pass through the following bead. Repeat this pattern, until you've worked completely around the beadwork in peyote stitch (figure 39). To begin the next round, step up by passing again through the first bead in the current round (figure 40).

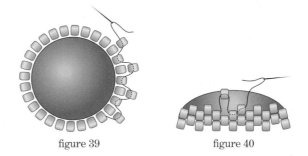

figure 39

figure 40

3 Peyote stitch the round. Repeat until you've worked completely around the beadwork. As you did previously, step up for the next round.

4 To tighten up the bezel around the component, switch to smaller beads, such as 15°s, for the final row when the bezel begins to flare out (figure 41).

figure 41

Odd-Count Peyote stitch Bezel

If you're unable to backstitch an even number of beads around the component, stitch on an odd number and proceed as in the even-count peyote bezel, except don't step up at the end of each round.

BACKING THE BEADWORK

Starting in the center and working your way outward, apply glue to the back of the beadwork on the foundation, leaving 3/16 inch (5 mm) free of glue all around the edge. You'll stitch through the edge to finish it; therefore, you don't want glue interfering with the process. Press the wrong side of the outer backing against the foundation. Allow the glue to dry; then trim the outer backing to the shape of the foundation.

Soutache Embroidery

With its sinuous curves, soutache jewelry looks complex to make, but really, it only requires a few basic stitching and beading techniques. You'll be amazed by how easy it is!

STITCHING

Unless the instructions tell you differently, work with the entire length of soutache you have on hand. If you do need to cut a piece to a specific length, the instructions will tell you to do so.

If you're adding additional layers of trim to an element you've already constructed, you can cut them to the length of the initial piece. Don't sew more than two layers of soutache together at once.

Whenever you begin to stitch, leave 2 inches (5.1 cm) of unattached allowance. It's essential to sew with small, regular stitches. You'll want to use a sharp needle and stick it precisely through the groove in the soutache, making sure not to hook or pull any of the threads that are part of the trim. If you're not happy with the way your stitching looks, gently rip it out and start over, using a new piece of soutache; unpicked trim looks damaged.

1 Thread your needle with a single strand of thread and knot one end.

2 Arrange the pieces of soutache so that they face the same direction. Tack them together with a few close, side-by-side stitches, hiding the knot between the layers of trim.

3 Bring your needle out of the trim, placed exactly in the groove.

4 Stick the needle precisely back in the same spot, and pass it through both layers of soutache at a slight angle so that it exits the last piece of trim exactly in the groove (figure 42).

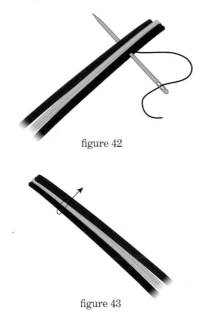

figure 42

figure 43

5 Keeping your stitches small and straight, repeat steps 3 and 4 as you stitch your way along the seam (figure 43).

If the thread becomes too short or if you finish sewing, draw your needle to the back of the work. Instead of making a knot, fasten the thread by making a few tight parallel stitches, keeping them as hidden as possible. Apply a drop of glue on these stitches to secure the thread.

FINISHING THE ENDS OF SOUTACHE

When you get to the end of a seam, fold the ends of the soutache to the back of the work and figure out where you want to trim them off. The ends of soutache have a tendency to fray. To prevent that, treat the ends with glue *before* cutting the soutache, as follows.

1 Soak the soutache with adhesive at the spot you intend to cut (figure 44).

figure 44

figure 45

2 As soon as the soutache starts to dry, trim the ends to get a clean, precise cut; then stitch down the ends on the back of the beadwork (figure 45).

ATTACHING SOUTACHE AROUND A BEAD

1 Because that tiny knot in your thread can pull through the trim, be sure to secure it with an initial blocking stitch as follows. Insert the needle through the trim from the outside (figure 46), stitch back through from the inside, and complete the blocking stitch by inserting the needle back through the soutache from the outside once again (figure 47).

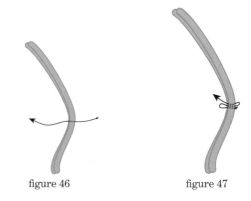

figure 46   figure 47

2 With the thread coming out of the groove in the soutache, string on a bead, wrap the soutache around it, and poke your needle through the soutache (figure 48).

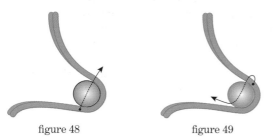

figure 48   figure 49

3 Take your needle back through the bead, poking it close to the spot from which the thread is exiting (figure 49).

4 Wrap the soutache completely around the bead and poke the needle through at the exact spot where the soutache meets the hole in the bead (figure 50).

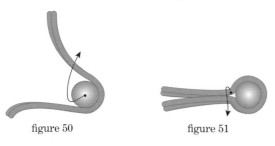

figure 50   figure 51

5 Secure both layers of soutache together below the bead with a few stitches (figure 51).

To add additional rows of soutache, be careful to always stitch through the groove in the trim (figure 52). Remember, add only one layer at a time! After stitching all the way around, tack the layers of the soutache together at the base of the bead with a few stitches (figure 53).

figure 52   figure 53

TIP

If you're stitching a row of beads to a component that you made in a previous step, always work with the needle coming out of the back of the work and stitch through as many of the existing layers as possible. Your stitches will be hidden later when you attach the backing.

ATTACHING SOUTACHE TO A CABOCHON

For a round or oval cabochon, mark the four cardinal points on the base material. You'll begin attaching the soutache at one of these points and end there as well (figure 54).

figure 54

1 Cement the flat bottom of the cabochon to a piece of fray-resistant base fabric, such as synthetic suede or beading foundation. After the adhesive has dried, trim away the base material to 1/8 inch (3 mm) all the way around.

2 After you thread the needle, pass it through the back of the base fabric so it comes up right next to the cabochon.

3 Poke the needle right into the groove of the piece of soutache that you wish to attach. Remember to leave 2 inches (5.1 cm) of unattached allowance, as shown in figure 55.

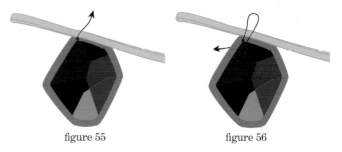

figure 55   figure 56

4 Making a stitch 1/16 to 1/8 inch (1.6 to 3 mm) long, bring the needle back through the soutache and the base fabric, close to the cab (figure 56).

5 As you keep repeating steps 3 and 4 to attach the soutache all around the cabochon, make sure the trim is held firmly against its edge (figure 57).

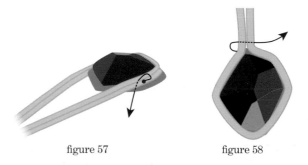

figure 57   figure 58

After you've finished, attach the two layers of soutache to one another with a few stitches (figure 58).

EDITOR
Nathalie Mornu

TECHNICAL EDITOR
Peggy Wright

EDITORIAL ASSISTANCE
Dawn Dillingham
Rebecca Shipkosky

ART DIRECTOR
Kathleen Holmes

COVER DESIGNER
Jo Obarowski

PRODUCTION
Kay Holmes Stafford

PHOTOGRAPHER
Lynne Harty

ILLUSTRATOR
Melissa Grakowsky Shippee

COVER IMAGE
Shutterstock

Index